HOW TO BUY OR LEASE A CAR WITHOUT GETTING RIPPED OFF

HOW TO BUY OR LEASE A CAR WITHOUT GETTING RIPPED OFF

by
Pique Lyle

Adams Media Corporation
Holbrook, Massachusetts

Published by
Adams Media Corporation
260 Center Street, Holbrook, MA 02343

ISBN: 1-58062-129-5

Printed in the United States of America.
J I H G F E D C B A

Library of Congress Cataloging-in-Publication Data

Lyle, P.K.
How to buy or lease a car without getting ripped off / by P.K. Lyle.
p.   cm.
Includes index.
ISBN 1-58062-129-5
1. Automobiles—Purchasing. 2. Automobile dealers. I. Title.
TLK162.L95   1999
629.222'029'6—dc21   98-49364
CIP

This publication is designed to provide accurate and authoritative information with regard to the subject matter covered. It is sold with the understanding that the publisher is not engaged in rendering legal, accounting, or other professional advice. If legal advice or other expert assistance is required, the services of a competent professional person should be sought.
          — From a *Declaration of Principles* jointly adopted by a Committee of the American Bar Association and a Committee of Publishers and Associations

Some of the names used in these stories have been changed.

Cover photo by George Pizzo.
Interior illustrations by Dot Bodiroga.

This book is available at quantity discounts for bulk purchases.
For information, call 1-800-872-5627 (in Massachusetts, 781-767-8100).

Visit our home page at http://www.adamsmedia.com

I wish to dedicate this book to anyone who has ever been victimized by the automotive world. Hopefully consumers will wise up and the victimizing will become a thing of the past. Yesterday wouldn't be soon enough!

CONTENTS

Preface

Did you ever wonder how two people who bought identical vehicles at the same time could walk away with deals that were so different? It most likely has to do with the knowledge that the buyers have before they walk into the showroom. Most people leave a tremendous amount of money "on the table" for the dealer, and it just isn't necessary. Frankly, purchasing a vehicle today is far more complex than it should be. There are so many tricks of the trade and things to watch for. Because of the Truth in Information Act, it's all in the fine print, but people seldom read it.

I will guide readers through the notorious maze of buying a vehicle intelligently and at great savings to the buyer by utilizing and applying my thirteen years of experience and memorable events as a sales representative, sales manager, and finance manager. Each one of you will be able to approach a purchase with much more knowledge, understanding, and confidence, thus better equipped to beat the dealer at his own games and drive that best bargain home.

Car dealers won't be happy to have this information exposed and so readily available, for they will be forced to become much more customer-oriented as their per-unit-profitability erodes and crumbles. If dealers continue to be resistant and demeaning, more and more consumers will turn to new and used automotive pricing and consulting services, auto club services, buyer agents, and the wonderful worldwide information highway, the Internet. My motivation to leave the car business? I was totally disgusted with the absurd and unjust games played upon good, hard-working people. I could not bear to watch any more souls get boldly slaughtered simply because they weren't informed—especially women!

> I believe that we're all winners and that we were put on this earth to help and love one another, (not hurt, steal, and cheat each other). For it is within each of us to rise above all evil and whatever hardships we've been dealt.

Take Notice

No, this is not another one of those boring, complicated, put-you-to-sleep annually published literary works filled with statistics, ratios, and complicated charts that will be obsolete almost as fast as you read it. And no, it's not a macho locker room book filled with few facts and a whole lot of slang and overused triteness written by some non-industry person who hired a research team to gather all the information. Bookstores, libraries, and racks everywhere are overflowing with these kinds of books and reference guides. Who's to say which ones are really the best? Some are inflated, some are deflated, but most definitely they become outdated.

This book is straight from the heart, written out of concern and compassion. I will lead you through the processes of shopping, buying, financing, and leasing automobiles in a manner that is easy to follow and understand. Unethical techniques and ridiculous game plans used by the retail automotive industry as well as their unbelievably disrespectful perspective towards customers are revealed. Remember, I worked in the business for thirteen long years. I know.

On the brighter side—the text is filled with colorful, "off the wall," tongue-in-cheek humor and musical overtones, the makings for a truly enjoyable book. There are lots of stories and the cartoon characters bring the topics to life in a highly amusing fashion. And speaking of life, I try to deliver strong survival messages of strength, courage, wisdom, understanding, patience, confidence, and hope. I want you to carry these messages with you not only when buying a vehicle, but throughout your entire life.

Acknowledgments

I'd like to thank my husband, Dick, my father (God rest his soul), my mother, my brother, Bubby, and my beautiful children. My family, my inner circle, were all very supportive during the process of writing this book.

In addition I'd like to thank my friends and colleagues who encouraged and guided me through this process: Ben Deering; Bob DiForio, my agent; Doug Friedman; Daryl Ostopowich; John Perri; and Rena Wolner. A special thanks to Dot Bodiroga, the illustrator of the book. The refreshingly different and funny illustrations make the book complete.

I'd like to thank Dr. James Johnson—thanks for the vision, Doc.

I'd like to thank everyone at Adams Media Corporation, especially Publisher Bob Adams. Thanks to the Publicity Department, Carrie Lewis and Rachel Pylant and a very special thanks to Jere Calmes, my editor.

Introduction

The Frog and the Scorpion

A friend once told me that buying a car reminded him about the tale of the frog and the scorpion. The scorpion approaches the frog and asks for a ride across the pond. The frog points out that he really isn't excited about carrying the scorpion across the pond on his back for scorpions are known to sting and kill. The scorpion persists in his request and becomes more persuasive to the point where the frog relents. The scorpion hops on the frog's back and they set out across the pond. Toward the middle of the pond, the frog feels a sharp pain in his back. Knowing full well

FROG AND THE SCORPION......
IT'S TIME TO TAKE THE STING AWAY

(·)'97 ©

> I always felt an enormous moral anguish when making thousands of dollars in profit on customers. At the same time if I didn't bleed them for every penny I could get, management would make me feel extremely inefficient and totally worthless to them, as though I hadn't done my job no matter how hard I tried.

that he has just been stung, he cries out to the scorpion. "What did you do that for? Now we will both surely die for you can't swim and you have stung me! Why?" The scorpion shrugs and replies, "I really don't know why. It's just my nature. That's what scorpions do!"

And so it is with auto dealers. They transform into scorpions and if given the opportunity, they will sting. It's just their nature. They are in business to sell, and they will present themselves in a gracious and helpful manner, but as a rule, a dealer's main interest above all else is to make the most profit they can on any given deal. As a customer, if you are not informed as to what all of your options are, a dealer will make more dollars off you than they will off someone who is informed. The person who is informed and drives a hard bargain will spend less than you will. It's a game of numbers and opportunity for dealers. You are a number and they are opportunists. They take advantage of circumstances—the circumstance being you don't know what you are doing or that you aren't as informed as you should be.

There are some dealers who are intentionally unscrupulous and have absolutely no compassion whatsoever when it comes to their customers and making the almighty dollar. Then there are those dealers who are just trying to do their job and make a good living at it. The fact remains though—dealers, managers, and sales representatives are all on the same team and if given an inkling of a chance, the scorpion will attack!

You don't have to carry that scorpion on your back. You can take him across the pond on your terms. You can coax that scorpion into a boat and pull him across! You will learn that the scorpion and the frog can both get what they want. Be cautious and use your head. When I began my career in the car business, it bothered me that one customer would buy a particular vehicle and pay $18,000 with no trade and the next customer buying an identical vehicle would pay only $15,000 with no trade! What was the difference? If you ask a dealer you will get some mumbo jumbo about different rebates, extra dealer discounts, etc., but the real bottom line is that the first customer was not as informed as the second customer. Dealers will make as much profit as you will allow them to make.

I used to be a scorpion, but now I am going to give the frogs a chance. It's time to take the sting away! I have done the very thing I'm warning against, but I am out of the car business now. I just couldn't continue being a scorpion. It was not possible for me to be totally truthful while working at a car lot and be a good employee at the same time.

I was between a rock and a hard place. I couldn't do a good job and feel good about it, so I quit.

As you will see, the favor she thought she was getting was anything but a favor.

One of My Most Haunting Memories as the Scorpion

One of my most haunting and perhaps most remorseful memories of my scorpion days is one that involved a very troubled woman (whom I'll call Cheryl). She had just gone through what seemed like seven years of bad luck—divorce, loss of income, and bankruptcy. Cheryl turned to our dealership for help but did we help her? NO!

She had been working as a part-time cosmetic consultant in order to earn a little extra spending cash while she was still married. But when the divorce took place and her situation changed, she had to work full-time. Cheryl had built a large clientele so the transition from part-time

> It was too late. I had already been stricken with the BLOOD-THIRSTY greed-demon and had transformed into a "scorpion."

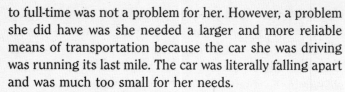

to full-time was not a problem for her. However, a problem she did have was she needed a larger and more reliable means of transportation because the car she was driving was running its last mile. The car was literally falling apart and was much too small for her needs.

The existing circumstances hindered the car buying process and made it difficult for Cheryl to attain a loan. Everything that she and her husband, (whom I'll call Michael), had ever bought was in his name with the exception of a few credit cards. Credit cards usually weren't considered substantial credit sources and all of the current finance programs for "high risk" customers that are prevalent today were still in the development stages. Her personal bank wouldn't loan her the money, so the dealer stepped in. (I was working as both sales manager and finance manager because the dealership was short handed at the time).

Michael was close friends with Jim, the owner of the dealership, so there were bitter feelings in the air. The entire situation was very awkward! Anyway, Jim agreed to help Cheryl get approved for a loan. He saw a huge opportunity to take advantage of someone that trusted him and he jumped on it. She picked out a brand new Chevy Celebrity wagon (perfect for delivering packages) and she drove it home that same day.

Cheryl came to us for help, right? We put her into the new car she needed, but we certainly did her no favors. Because Jim personally handled the approval of the financing, he sold the car at the price and payment he wanted and basically told her, this is the price and this is the payment. No negotiating. Take it or leave it. She took it (like she had a big choice?) The purchase price was $2,000 over the manufacturer's sticker price and reflected a marked-up dealer addendum sticker full of fluff and puff.

The finance terms were for seventy-two months at 19 percent interest, which was the state maximum rate charge allowed for that number of months on new automobiles. The payment included credit life, accidental health insurance, and an extended warranty marked up $1,000 over our cost.

When Jim brought me the deal, I just about flipped. I called him into a different office so that she couldn't hear our conversation. I literally begged him not to do this to her and pointed out that the divorce was between Cheryl and Michael, not Cheryl and Jim. He told me to shut up and process the deal or get the hell out (as in fired!).

Looking back, I should have walked into my office, grabbed Cheryl and my personal belongings, and left, never to return. But I didn't. There was too much commission to give up and I didn't want to lose any future commissions either. My heart said no but my brain justified it. After all, I had to make a living. I had bills to pay.

Basically, we slaughtered her. That particular deal made the dealership about $8,000 profit and we certainly didn't help Cheryl. We only added to her troubles. About eighteen months later, she lost the car because she couldn't afford the high payments any longer. If I could turn back the clock, I would in a split second! This memory will haunt me forever.

> The scorpions attacked and the frog drowned.

First Impressions

Before you step out that front door, you'd better take a good look in the mirror. What do you see? How do you look? How do you smell? Are your clothes clean and pressed if needed? I hope you're not wearing dirty, smelly sneakers! Is your breath offensive? And are you having a bad hair day? Time out!

Whether one wants to admit it or not, FIRST IMPRES-SIONS are extremely important and your appearance will have an effect on the way you are received and treated not only at the dealership, but in life in general.

When buying an automobile, a bad first impression can overshadow your deal, casting difficulty on coming to terms with the dealer, thus costing you money. So make sure you always look your very best before approaching any sales force. Dress it up and make yourself as attractive as possible, but do it in good taste and don't go overboard. No nightclub glitz and glitter, you might give them the wrong impression. Whether you're male or female, wear your best fragrance, the kind that makes one drool and melt to the floor. (Careful though. Too much of a good thing can be bad). And turn on the charm.

These efforts will bring out that certain element of sensuality that's within each of us, thus creating a distraction and loss of concentration and a weakened sales force, if you know what I mean. That's just what you want because it will subconsciously break down their guard and your chances of getting a better deal are increased. Work it to your benefit and break them down right from the get-go. I know this sounds absolutely crazy but it's the human truth. We're human and it's our humanly nature. Just a thought!

On the other hand, sometimes our appearance cannot be helped, and even in those cases, the retail world can be very cruel. I once had a neighbor friend, Ralph, who was dying from cancer and had been in the hospital for several days receiving chemotherapy treatments. Before being dismissed, he made the decision to leave his family a new car and as soon as he was released, he went car shopping.

Ralph could have been spotted a mile away. He was truly a character to be remembered. He always wore his favorite bright red baseball cap that had to be pried from his head. His personal hygiene wasn't exactly up to par because he had just gotten out of the hospital. He had a scraggly beard from not shaving for days. His wardrobe consisted of wrinkled bib overalls and an old suit jacket. That's what he had on when he was admitted to the hospital. The chemo delivery tube was still dangling from his nose. The doctors left it intact because Ralph had to undergo more chemo treatments. Well, I think you can visualize him quite vividly. But above all, tucked away inside those overalls was a large roll of thousand dollar bills! Ralph always had money and plenty of it.

He was very partial to Cadillacs so it was natural for him to head to the nearest Cadillac dealership. Guess what? Nobody would wait on him. They avoided him like a plague. He tried another Cadillac dealership and experienced the same thing. Not a soul would give him the time of day. Ralph got angry and decided to head for the Chrysler dealer, thinking that the Chrysler New Yorker or Fifth Avenue would make a good substitute for a Cadillac. Well, nobody there would help him either. So off he went to the Lincoln dealer, which just happened to be on his way home. By now he was not only extremely upset, but also severely fatigued.

He lucked out though. Ralph drove home that day in a brand new, loaded-to-the-hilt Lincoln Town Car. He thought about how stupid and ignorant the sales people from the other dealerships would feel if they had only known about the wad of money in his pocket. They prejudged him based on his clothing and his looks. Oh well, their loss.

Someone at the Lincoln dealership accepted Ralph's odd appearance. Someone treated him with respect. Someone made an easy sale because they didn't judge him and took time to get beyond his appearance. God bless that individual.

On a lighter and funnier note, I'll never forget about the time this pig farmer came into the dealership

First
impressions
are lasting
impressions.

wearing his work coveralls. The odor from his clothing was repulsive! It was the most horrible scent I believe I have ever smelled in my entire life! It was all I could do to keep from losing my lunch. Anyway, it took about one second for the pig odor to permeate the entire showroom and everyone, including me, took off running back into the service department to hide. We were like a bunch of little kids. Nobody wanted to wait on this poor man because he smelled so bad. He must have stood in the showroom for at least twenty minutes before Steve, the service manager, walked up to wait on him. (Steve knew him—that's why he waited on him.) That was until he picked out a new SUV (Sports Utility Vehicle), and then Steve turned him over to me to write the deal up. He was mine, odor and all. I took him into my office, wrote up the deal, and began processing the loan. He wanted to finance through the manufacturer on their special low advertised finance rate.

After about five minutes I had to excuse myself—I couldn't stand it any longer. I went and got a fan that was stored back in the parts department and brought it to my office. I was so embarrassed but I couldn't help it. I plugged it in proclaiming to be hot and tried to blow all the stinky air out of there. It didn't work. Finally, after about another five minutes and barely able to breathe, I asked him to please wait in the showroom and I'd bring the papers to him.

He took delivery of his SUV and from that day forward, every time he showed up, we all ran to hide as fast as we could. Were we bad? WE WERE B-A-D! What can I say? First impressions are lasting impressions.

I swear, my office smelled like pigs for a month!

Some Things to Know Before Setting Out to Shop

There are definitely some inside secrets you must know before setting out to shop. For instance, when you go to an auto dealership, it's possible to buy a used vehicle that is being sold as new! One particular incident really stands out in my mind.

It was a beautiful spring afternoon and the dealership was receiving a shipment of conversion minivans. All of a sudden one of them did a major nosedive off the transport truck while being unloaded. There were some extensive damages but since the transport company was responsible for the incident, the dealer had no worries. He put the van in the body shop to be repaired and when all repairs were completed, the van was flawless. It was stocked into inventory and on with business as usual.

Technically, a dealer can sell it as new because the vehicle has never been titled, even though it has been in the body shop for three weeks being repaired. Is that what you want to buy? Especially if you are paying the same price as for one that has never been damaged! Eventually some poor clueless soul bought it and paid an absolute fortune for it without ever being told what had happened. Shocking isn't it?

It's hard to believe, but this sort of thing happens often. How about the "new" leftover model from the previous year that just happened to be in a flood or the one that has several thousand demo miles on it. Yes, dealers will mislead you and sell them to you new—but they're not

> Watch out! What will get you into trouble is not what you know, but rather what you don't know.

SHOCKING ISN'T IT

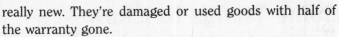

"Eany meany miny mo—is this the auto that I drove?"

really new. They're damaged or used goods with half of the warranty gone.

If the vehicle you decide to buy is one of several identical units, make sure you write down the VIN number (vehicle identification number) and the mileage before test-driving. The units may be identical in looks but one might actually be six months older, or have a higher mileage. The interior may be more worn or it could have had body damage at some point in time. There are numerous possibilities. The bottom line is this: When the sales representative takes "your car" back to the clean-up shop to be prepped for delivery, it may not be "your car." He/she will usually take the one they've had in stock the longest, or the one they have the least amount of money in. "Why not?" asks the dealer, "The customer will never know and it's a good way to add extra profit to the deal."

There is only one way to assure that what you think you are buying is indeed what you are really buying, and that is to collect as much reliable information as possible before setting out to shop and before committing to buy anything. I will do my very best to inform you as thoroughly as possible. You will learn how to successfully shop for deals on wheels and win. You can drive away with your next vehicle purchase feeling confident that you got fair value for your money. It doesn't matter if it is your first or your fiftieth purchase. Along with this information and a better understanding of how the car business works, I know you will get a much better deal.

Time and time again over a period of thirteen years I saw literally thousands of people of all ages, all races, and all income levels taken advantage of in the worst way. There were very few exceptions. Even a worldwide honored and acclaimed female TV personality that hosts her

own show, (whose name I'm not permitted to mention), has been slammed—*HARD!* I heard that out of her own mouth. I had just gotten home from picking my mother up at the airport. We turned the TV on to watch her show. The show was about saving money, and during the last segment they discussed buying cars. The host commented that she had recently bought a car thinking she had gotten this great deal. When everything was signed, sealed, and delivered, she ended up paying much more than the original price. I thought to myself, WOW! Even she was victimized! Just think what dealers do to the rest of us!

My mentioning this famous personality's unfortunate experience is to point out the general attitude in the retail automotive industry towards their customers, no matter what their position in life may be. And if a customer happens to be an uninformed woman and she comes into a dealership alone, she had best be prepared for attack! The dealer will attempt to take advantage of her.

Obviously, dealers (and their employees) would never admit to this. It's unfortunate that even in today's very modern world, much of our female population still turns to men for help when purchasing automobiles. For most, their overall knowledge is extremely limited. It doesn't have to be that way!

> Do not walk onto a car lot or into a showroom to buy a car until you are absolutely ready NOT to buy.

Don't Buy Until You're Ready Not to Buy

There is one single-most important point to remember about buying a vehicle. Above all else: Do not walk onto a car lot or into a showroom to buy a car until you are absolutely ready NOT to buy.

> If a woman comes in, especially by herself, she is the prey for the day!

Meaning simply this: You are in control. You've done your homework. You know what you want and understand your needs. You know your financial limits and what your options are. And finally, you are confident enough to walk away from a bad deal!

Special Note: You will notice throughout the entire book lots of repetition. By being repetitive, I hope you will not only better absorb the subject matter, but that it will grow to be a part of your everyday life, transforming you into a much stronger and more independent person in all that you do.

THE PREY..

CHAPTER 1

The Dealers

How much does a new automobile cost these days? The average buyer pays around $20,000 (give or take a little) for something he or she is unlikely to keep for more than sixty months at most. If there are two new automobiles in an average-income family, and both are financed, the total amount to be paid with interest will approach $50,000 or more. How much did you pay for your home? Do you want to save money on your next vehicle purchase? Have you any idea how many people are being taken every time they buy one?

With so many special programs available (many of which are quite complicated), consumers are continually getting the wool pulled over their eyes. It sure amazed me how many customers bought new vehicles and paid more than the sticker price. Supposedly the particular unit that they wanted was the very last one like it anywhere. Or, the truck they happened to pick out was in such great demand that dealers everywhere were selling them $3,000 and $4,000 over the MSRP (Manufacturer's Suggested Retail Price). Yeah right, and I own oceanfront property in the desert. A perfect example of this is the new craze for an old car. Volkswagen revamped the old VW Bug and brought it back to the public. It has been in such great demand that dealers are selling them for thousands over the sticker price. Even customers are buying them up and then turning right around and selling them for thousands over what they paid. The manufacturers can't do a thing about it

Even the Know-It-All and the so-called experienced buyer get financially raped!

either because factories cannot keep up with the demand for the Bug. (What are you willing to pay? How far are you willing to bend over for the dealer?)

I'll never forget about a particular 4x4 short-bed pickup truck that came in on shipment. I can still see it plain as day. I swear it was so bizarre, it looked like something straight out of the Dukes of Hazard show. This truck had great big spotlights all across the top. It had an added roll bar, dual rear wheels, red, white, and blue striped graphic designs, a CB radio with an antenna long enough to send electromagnetic waves all the way to the moon and back, and a bunch of other outlandish gadgets. The sales manager must have ordered it either as a joke or when he was half-cocked, if you know what I mean. You just don't order those kinds of units.

Anyway, it was such an unusual looking set of wheels that for fun we decided to drive it up onto a display rack that was outside on the front lawn of the dealership. To our surprise it didn't take but about five minutes for the rednecks to come crawling out from under the woodwork to check out Daisy. (That's what we called the truck). They were like bees swarming around a jar of honey. It was so unbelievably funny!

Because of the attraction that Daisy was drawing, guess what happened to the price? It went up, up, and up, and finally sold for $4,000 over the sticker price. The new owner was as happy as a puppy with his first doggie bone. Of course the reason we sold it at $4,000 over was because Daisy was one of a kind, a rare jewel, and everybody wanted her. We told the customer that if he really wanted the truck he was gonna have to fork it over right then and there at the price we demanded and not a penny less. He did. He bent way over! "Everybody wanted Daisy."

She was gonna sell quickly! Smells like that oceanfront property to me.

This customer was obviously not informed and acted on pure impulse. Big mistake! He fell hook, line, and sinker. Surprisingly, this type of incident occurs all the time. Many of my customers never questioned the price quoted to them, or asked if that was the best we could do! They just closed their eyes and bit the dust fearing any confrontation.

> Cha Ching, Cha Ching, Cha Ching! Another one bites the dust!

After the sale, customers would follow me to the finance office (mostly referred to as the business office so as not to intimidate the customer). They would proceed to part with more of their hard-earned money than necessary to pay for credit life and accidental health insurance at drastically inflated rates. Then they would buy extended warranties that would eventually prove to be either worthless or difficult to use should they ever seek to file a claim. Customers had no idea what was happening since the whole process was executed in such a professional manner.

People, please wake up! I want to see consumers walk up to a sales representative and get what they deserve at a dollar amount that is fair to all. Even with major price cuts, a dealer will continue to prosper. The sales team (including sales managers) will try to lay a major guilt trip on the customer. They would have you think they lost money. Don't believe them! They wouldn't sell you the vehicle if they weren't making money.

There's much more than meets the public eye, as I'll explain further into the book. Always remember that it's a numbers game. If dealers fail to profit as much as they would like on a given deal, they will attempt to slam dunk the next, and the next, and the next.

CHA CHING CHING CHING CHING oo....

> If the seller refuses, "Stop in the Name of Money."

If you follow the advice I'm offering, you can get the best deal that is possible. Dealers will still make a reasonable profit, which is what they are entitled to. I know all about free enterprise and how it works. Caveat emptor—let the buyer beware—and all that. Whatever the market will bear. I'll show you how to lower the amount that the market will bear by making you an informed buyer who knows what questions to ask and who recognizes the answers that are going to save you money!

Let's start with the basics. Most basic of all, where to go when you want to buy a new ride. There are many places to locate an automobile suitable for your needs and budget: large and small dealerships, used car lots of all sorts and sizes, buy-here pay-here lots, and individuals. I must warn you though, when buying from an individual, be wise and find someone competent to judge the mechanics and value of the vehicle.

Also, be positively sure it's not a hot piece of goods (stolen) before you hand over any cash! Get the vehicle identification number and have the local license bureau run a history/title check on it. The seller wants you to buy, but if you do, you have almost no recourse once the title is in your name. You must be allowed to have a reliable mechanic whom you trust evaluate the merchandise!

Since I mentioned hot goods, let me point out that it is easy to fall victim to this crime. It even happens to dealers.

A very young, inexperienced wealthy man whom I'll call John owned one of the dealerships that I worked for. He would rather have played weekend farm warrior than do anything else. He romanced the idea of farming. If the truth were known, John really wasn't interested in the dealership much at all, but it was a gift from his father for his twenty-first birthday. You see, he came from a long line of wealthy car dealers: his grandfather, his father, and his uncle. John never was really interested in the family business, so in hopes of changing that, his father bought him his very own dealership in a rural community. It was too long of a commute from the city to the dealership every day, so John had to move. He bought himself a big farm with a beautiful three-story home already built on it and moved to the country. The property also had two barns, several sheds, and was fenced in for livestock. Being the proud new owner of his own farm, he was anxious to fill the barns with farm equipment. Now the real story begins.

It was a slow weekend morning and we were all sitting around in the showroom waiting for some action. The sales manager and I both played guitar so every Saturday we would bring our guitars to work. It was our weekend morning ritual to pick 'n' grin, drink coffee, and eat donuts. We also grilled out a lot on weekends and, yes, customers were always welcome to partake of the feast if they so desired. Often they did. About halfway through the coffee and donuts we noticed a huge (and I mean huge) tractor blazing a trail across the lot. It was a farmer from the next county over wanting to trade his tractor in on a brand new Chrysler Fifth Avenue, loaded with every option available.

John decided to go ahead and trade with him. After all, he needed a tractor and that would be one less piece of farm equipment he would have to buy. The farmer told him that he did not have the title on the tractor with him but that he would bring it to the dealership within the next few days. They shook hands, did the paperwork, and the deal was done. The farmer went on his merry way driving his new car. Old John Boy couldn't have been happier. Immediately he drove the tractor over to his farm. Several days went by as did several phone calls.

> It was a farmer from the next county over wanting to trade his tractor in on a brand new Chrysler Fifth Avenue, loaded with every option available.

And several more days went by as did several more phone calls. The farmer was not to be found. This went on for a couple of weeks and then it happened. The FBI, half of the police department, and a helicopter flying overhead showed up at the dealership.

It turned out that the tractor was stolen merchandise and was part of an ongoing theft ring investigation. At first the authorities thought John was involved. We were literally freaking out because they were questioning all of us. I was the business manager and didn't sense anything wrong whatsoever. I thought it was just an honest, hard-working farmer wanting a new car. It seemed like a normal transaction with the exception that the trade was a tractor, but John would trade for anything with value. He traded for cattle, horses, boats, remodeling for his new house and even a brand new riding lawn mower from one of the local mom-and-pop hardware stores, which I ended up buying. If it had value, he would trade. The authorities seized the tractor and broke John's heart. In that short period of time, he had really grown fond of it. It was his first tractor for his new endeavors. But the big task was yet to come—finding the Fifth Avenue. The FBI did find the car about two months later. It was totally stripped for parts and burned.

What's my point in this whole tractor story and what does it have to do with anything? Well, if a dealer can fall victim to stolen property so easily, just think how easy it is for unsuspecting customers to fall victim to the same crime. Dishonesty flourishes throughout the automotive world, and hot merchandise is sold all the time. To beat it all, the one selling the hot goods won't even flinch during the process. So you see, one can never be too careful when buying an automobile, or in this case, trading for a tractor!

Step right up!

Big Volume Dealers

When the decision is made to go car shopping, many people start out at large dealerships on the main drag. Shopping at big volume stores does have certain advantages. You will be able to find practically any line and model of vehicle you wish to buy along with more of a selection to choose from, including the higher-priced and specialty units. This is the one place you can most likely buy at the best price, though there are no hard-and-fast rules. Big volume dealers will drop the price quicker than the little guys, but will also be more willing to let a customer walk if they don't get the price they want. They know that if they miss a sale there's always another one waiting in line. Your results are going to be up to you and your ability to remember and utilize the information in this book.

The philosophy of all new car dealers is to sell as many units as possible at a profit and to maintain a high Customer Satisfaction Index. CSI is the rating on which quality of product and service to customers is based. Units sold and CSI ratings directly affect the existence of dealerships, their inventory, and what is allocated (distributed) to them by the manufacturers. If the number of units sold and CSI ratings fall too low, dealers could be penalized, lose incentives, or perhaps, even lose their franchise. With higher sales and higher ratings, their status with manufacturers not only increases, but they will also receive even more of the "higher priced" and "specialty" automobiles for their inventory. Dealerships, especially large ones, work

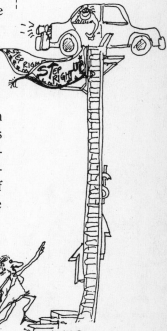

May the best man (or woman) win!

aggressively to attain these popular units because, like a circus attraction, they most definitely draw a big crowd.

Particularly among large dealerships, owners and sales management teams battle to win factory sponsored sales awards, cash bonuses, and trips. Therefore, they foster an energized atmosphere of extreme competitiveness. They are usually quicker and more willing to negotiate than smaller dealerships simply because they sell more units. But at the end of each month when the heat is on and the race is almost over, everybody wants that last and final sale.

Sales managers will be attempting to reach sales quotas by moving as many units as possible so as not to fall short of contest requirements and company goals. Sales representatives are most often paid on a draw against commission (percent of profit) unless they work for a Saturn dealership in which they are paid a regular salary. A draw is a set dollar amount paid weekly. At month end, the total draw is deducted from total commissions and the balance is paid. If sales representatives are having a slow month, they will be anxious to have your deal in their pocket. More sales equal fatter paycheck and commission percentages, which normally increase based on the number of units sold in that month.

Then there's the mini-deal, which usually pays around $50.00 to $75.00 in commission. A mini-deal is one in which little or no profit is made. A sales rep is guaranteed a certain amount of commission on a mini-deal.

By the way, for those of you who have ever thought about automotive sales as a career, here's a little insight you might want to consider first. There's a huge turnover. The unfortunate dark reality of being in automotive sales is that not only is it a cut-throat business, but the hours are notoriously long. If you don't move units and you

MAY THE BEST "MAN OR WOMAN" WIN.....

don't produce profit, you're out! You're fired no matter how hard you've tried! As for the mini-deals, too many "pocket-breakers" and you're out the door.

When a woman starts making more than the guy(s) or begins climbing that ladder, grab your shield. Darts are gonna fly. This is another one of those ugly truths that will never be admitted. Unfortunately as we enter the new millennium, the retail auto industry is still ruled by men and they want to keep it that way.

I was continually harassed, told that all women were good for was "you know" and having babies, and that a woman's place was at home with her husband and kids, not selling cars and certainly not in management. Also the principles of justice and equality were thrown out the window. At one of the dealerships I worked for as a finance manager, I had about 100 deals stolen right out from under my nose. Because the other finance manager (who happened to be a man) was complaining that I was making more money than he was, he threatened to quit. Because he was such a good buddy with the general manager, the general manager instructed all sales personnel to turn 75 percent of their customers over to him, taking away a big percentage of my customers. It took me about two months to figure out what was going on and finally, when I confronted one of the sales representatives, he confessed to the scheme. Needless to say, this really hurt deeply in more ways than one.

Another dealer that I worked for, also as a finance manager, screwed me out of a one-week, all-expenses-paid trip for two to Hawaii. I had won the trip by selling the most extended warranties/service contracts for our region within a given period of time. I was totally thrilled because I had never been there before. Unfortunately, the dealer told me that I couldn't go at the designated time.

For example:
Units = % profit, 1–5 units = 15%, 6–10 units = 20%, 11–15 units = 25%, 16–20 units = 30%, etc.

If you're a woman in the business, that's another whole book in itself. Be prepared for all kinds of harassment from sexual to racial, and expect discrimination, especially if you become successful.

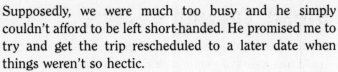

Supposedly, we were much too busy and he simply couldn't afford to be left short-handed. He promised me to try and get the trip rescheduled to a later date when things weren't so hectic.

That was the last I ever heard about any trip except that coincidentally his newlywed son and daughter-in-law went to Hawaii on their honeymoon at the exact same time that I was supposed to go, and of course, all of their expenses were paid. It doesn't take a rocket scientist to figure that one out.

In a nutshell, the car business can be a very unfair, unjust, and sometimes heartbreaking way to make a living. I would think about it long and hard before ever venturing down that avenue.

Now, back to our discussion of big volume dealers. Large dealers obviously have larger inventories. Factory finance companies and other financial lenders supply the funds to dealers for their inventory. This is called floor-planning. Floorplanning is an ongoing process. A dealer pays interest monthly on units in stock, and as the units are sold the financial lenders are paid off.

Fast-moving inventory is great for everybody from the owners and employees of dealerships to the owners and employees of automotive manufacturers. This makes it possible for the salesforce to work with new and fresh stock on a regular basis and secures thousands of manufacturing jobs. Nothing is worse for a dealer than to be stuck with a bunch of leftover models at the end of the year.

You can sometimes get a great price on these units if that's what you want, but don't be surprised when you apply for a loan and the lender refuses to give you all the money you need. Even though the car is new, it's still considered a year old once the new current year models are out.

Small Volume Dealers

Small dealerships can offer great prices also and they aren't only found in small towns. They're everywhere. The inventory will obviously be smaller, but don't let what you see on their lot fool you. Small dealers occasionally will have storage lots located nearby, and they can always find what you want on the Locator (a computer service utilized by dealers to find the vehicle you want). The locator will search dealer inventories all over the United States. The dealer will try to stay within his geographical region, however, because of the added costs of paying someone to go get the unit from another dealer, plus road expenses such as gas, food, and hotel. These additional charges are added to your deal.

The small dealer will generally be more difficult to negotiate with on price but will view you more as a valued customer, versus the large dealer generally viewing you more as a number. The little guys have to make more per unit than the big guys because they have fewer sales, less inventory to work with, fewer incentives and spiffs, and less consumer traffic. Even though they are not as quick to drop the price, in the end they are less likely to let a customer walk because of price. With fewer customers they need every sale they can get.

It's a great feeling to be personally valued. In many cases the small dealer won't have the lowest price, yet they won't be very far off from the large dealer's price either, and that, combined with the friendly atmosphere, makes the small dealer competitive. The small dealer is often a long-time family-owned store and depends greatly on repeat business and referrals.

> The very fact that a smaller dealer identifies you as an individual with a name as opposed to a "small fish in a big sea" may make it a viable place for you to shop.

"What's behind door number 1,2, and 3?" Sound familiar?

Without repeat business and referrals, the business could dwindle away to nothing. With the large dealer, again it's numbers. You have to weigh the difference. A valued-customer or just another statistic?

What to Look for in the Service Department

The service department can tell you quite a bit about a dealership. Is it well lit and clean? If so, it's a fair indication that the shop is professionally managed and staffed. It reflects pride of workmanship. It shows that the owner and management of the dealership cares about having you as a customer long after the initial sale. The same thing holds true if it's messy. A sloppy place (sludgy, slimy gook everywhere) equals sloppy management. If a dealer doesn't permit a service department tour, red lights should start flashing! There are insurance regulations concerning customers in a shop, but you just want to see it, not work in it. So does it matter all that much? You better believe it!

The service department will become the representative of the dealership once you drive off the lot in that shiny new ride. This is where warranty work, general maintenance, and other mechanical repairs are done. I know customers who have been perfectly happy with their purchase and the dealership until they had to deal with the service department. It was here the relationship with the dealer turned into a nightmare. Little problems like seats with strange bumps in them that only the owner seems to be able to notice but that make the vehicle a torture chamber. Taking it in for one repair and three repairs are made without the customer's approval. Fixing a

Door # 1,2,3 - SATISFIED CUSTOMERS

problem and the problem is not fixed. It doesn't stop there! If this situation occurs and isn't handled to the owner's satisfaction either because of incompetence or a don't-give-a-X#!0 attitude, as a customer, you can have a short relationship with the dealership and the memory will last a lifetime!

On the other hand, if all problems are dealt with quickly and by knowledgeable and caring employees, the dealer will have gained a lifelong friend and an advertising source of the very best kind—a satisfied customer!

Dealers that really care about their business will take pride in keeping the door of communication open between themselves, the sales team, the service department team, and most importantly, their customers. Remember CSI? They will see to it that the service department looks clean and organized and is staffed with intelligent and well-qualified people. That is not to say that the shop won't have lots of activity, but in spite of the activity, you will notice that all is running smoothly. Repairing automobiles is obviously not the world's cleanest endeavor. However, when it's time to go home, the mess will be gone.

So look around before you stroll into the showroom. Realize that you're not only buying a vehicle, but service as well. Check out the service department and talk to the service manager. Determine if he's someone you could relate to. Are you treated with respect when you are not yet a customer? If not, what are the chances that will change when you do become a customer?

I would suggest not going first thing Monday morning when the

> The sales department performs the ceremony. The service department is supposed to keep you happily married!

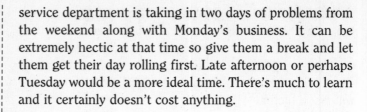

service department is taking in two days of problems from the weekend along with Monday's business. It can be extremely hectic at that time so give them a break and let them get their day rolling first. Late afternoon or perhaps Tuesday would be a more ideal time. There's much to learn and it certainly doesn't cost anything.

What to Look for in the Parts Department

Walk over toward the parts department and observe what goes on there. Is it busy? Do people get what they need in fast order or are they out of stock on everything? (You don't want to be stranded without wheels waiting for the stork to deliver your specially ordered overdue part, do you?) If that's the case, maybe the dealership is having financial difficulties.

Unless it's close to inventory time, when companies purposefully let inventory levels drop for tax reasons, a solid dealer will keep in stock a wide array of parts for all the different models of his lines (Chevy, Olds, Toyota, Honda, etc.). That doesn't mean that he'll have a widget for a 1928 Puttmobile, but he will have an idler arm for his 1996 Taurus wagon if he's a Ford dealer.

Some of the larger dealerships will have a huge parts store that sells parts, automotive products, and accessories to other dealers all across the country and to the public. The smaller dealerships usually service their own local area.

Make inquiries and observations but do not be a pest. Employees have a job to do. If they have a day to kill, it might be wise to check out some other locations.

What to Look for in the Body Shop

One more thing to consider when selecting a dealership is whether it has a body shop. It's comforting to know that if you or someone in your family is involved in an automobile accident, all you have to do is make a phone call to the dealer and help is on the way. They will usually send a wrecker right over and you will probably be able to get a loaner car immediately. The body shop will repair your automobile if it isn't totaled unless you choose to go elsewhere.

By the way, as a general rule body shop employees of a new dealership are highly skilled and most often factory-trained as a requirement of their employment. The body shop must be able to produce top-quality repairs that can't be detected by a potential customer. If your vehicle is beyond repair, the body shop manager will refer you to the sales department for further assistance.

While we're on the topic of body shops, some of the shady tactics used to increase profits are unbelievable. Millions of dollars are pocketed every year because of bogus bodywork. Talk about tricks of the trade and falsified estimates! You might find this next little section very disturbing.

Bogus Bodywork (How to Make Big Bucks with Shady Tactics)

- After a customer has dropped off their vehicle to be repaired or after it has been towed in, (so that the customer does not see it again until after repairs are made), they will drive the car into a wall or another vehicle. This increases

OF COURSE ANY GUILTY PARTY, WHETHER IT BE A CAR DEALER, BODY SHOP OWNER, SHOP MANAGER, OR INSURANCE ADJUSTER, WOULD BE IN COMPLETE DENIAL . . .

WELL?

the damages, thus getting more money out of the insurance company. This is *usually* unbeknownst to the owner.

- To make the appearance of frame damage, they will loosen a door hinge so that the gap at the top of the door is wide and at the bottom is narrow. This suggests to the adjuster that the frame is damaged thus increasing the estimate.

- If the automobile is supposed to get new parts, they will take the parts off, clean them up, straighten them and/or paint them to make them look new and pocket the money. Usually the customer cannot tell the difference.

- If the vehicle was hit in the front, they will remove a hubcap, take the wheel off and place one or two washers between the rim and the drum, and then put the wheel and hubcap back on. They spin the tire in the adjuster's presence and it wobbles giving the appearance of bent parts (bigger bucks!). They will also let the air out of the tire. This would justify the need for a front wheel alignment, a new tire, and new parts.

- For photograph requirements: Thin pin-striping tape is placed on a fiberglass body or on the windshield. In a picture, it shows up looking just like cracks in the body or in the windshield.

- Quarter panels are expensive to replace. They will get paid for a new one but will straighten the old one instead and pocket the money. This applies to any parts that can be straightened.

- Hood hinges are loosened to give the appearance of sprung hinges. "Sprung hinges" have to be replaced, don't they?

- If the car was hit in the rear and there are supposed to be new parts replaced in the trunk, the old ones are straightened instead and black undercoating is sprayed over them to cover the fake repairs giving the appearance of new parts.
- They will loosen the bumper on one side so that it hangs down giving the appearance of broken parts.
- They will pop the molding from around the windshield and strike the edge of the windshield to create a crack. This gives the appearance of a harder impact.
- If the car was hit in the front, the air conditioning lines are loosened so that all of the Freon will leak out giving the appearance of a hole in the coil or cracked lines. Must replace those parts!
- For photograph requirements: Headlights will be smashed in order to get paid for a complete new headlight assembly. Actually, this applies to anything that can be smashed or bent to increase the estimate.

Bogus bodywork hardly scratches the surface of the many ongoing devious practices which in reality are fraudulent insurance claims. Can you imagine what this does to your insurance premium? It goes up! So if you're ever involved in a wreck, pay close attention to detail. Try to find out exactly what condition your automobile is in as soon as possible and if you can, take pictures before it is driven or towed away. Make sure you get the repairs that you or your insurance company has paid for. You're better off going to someone that you know really well and can trust. Even then, be careful. Surprise insurance bills are never pleasant!

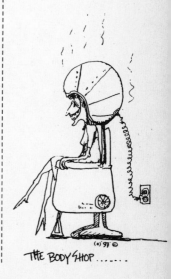

THE BODY SHOP........

CHAPTER 2

You, the Customer

Prior to venturing out into the automotive world for that exciting shopping spree, not only should you pay attention to your appearance, but certain forethought should take place and proper procedures should be known and understood to the best of your ability. It is far too risky to not be totally prepared for what is about to unfold. If you were taking a college course exam, wouldn't you study hard and try to absorb as much information about the subject as possible prior to the exam? Of course you would! The same attitude and effort should be applied when purchasing an automobile. It's homework time! Believe me, if a salesperson senses any weakness at all, you'll be that frog drowning from the scorpion's poisonous sting of death!

What to Consider Before You Go

Before beginning your quest, you should make some decisions (or at least be fairly close to making decisions). For example: What price range do you want to consider and how are you going to pay for your purchase? Are you financing/leasing or can you pay cash? If so, will it be through an automotive factory source or leasing company, a bank the dealer processes his customer loans through, or will you go through your own personal bank or credit union? Who can get the best interest rate, you or the dealer? Should you go with a fixed rate or a variable rate and which one is better? The fixed rate remains constant throughout the loan but the variable rate fluctuates. It might decrease or it might increase, depending on what the prime rate does. Chapter 7 will give a more in-depth look at interest rates.

Down Payment

How much of a down payment is required, if any at all? The down payment requirement usually depends on one's past credit history. If the dealership is handling your financing, the finance manager (also referred to as the business manager so as not to intimidate the customer) will try to get as much down-stroke (down payment) out of you as possible. The more down-stroke you have, the more equity (ownership) you will have and the lower your payment will be. That's great, but understand that the finance manager is going to try and convince you to buy credit life and accidental health insurance and extended warranty, which hikes your payment right back up there.

What's Your Limit?

I can't stress enough how important it is for you to know what your financial limit is before walking into the showroom and especially before walking into the business office. How much can you afford and do you have excellent credit, marginal credit, poor credit, or nonexistent credit? Excellent credit is when a customer has paid every payment on time for any financial obligation they might have had whether it is a loan or a credit card. Marginal credit is when a customer has had some problems making payments on time but is still a valid risk. Poor credit is when a customer has had many problems making payments on time, collections, liens or judgements filed against them, had a repossession, or even filed bank-

ruptcy. Finally, nonexistent credit is simply that: customers who have never borrowed any money nor have ever had any credit cards of their own. You've got to have a plan.

Type/Add-Ons

What make of vehicle do you want—domestic or foreign? What type of vehicle do you want (economy, family, sports, luxury, sports utility, 2x4, 4x4, or all-wheel drive)? How about traction control? Do you need a two-door or a four-door and how do you want it equipped? Do you want it basic, or do you want every possible option available to mankind? Do you want a four-, six-, or eight-cylinder engine? And of course, what about the transmission? There are four- and five-speed manual transmissions, and automatic transmissions. There are power steering, power brakes, power windows, power door locks, power seats (cloth, vinyl, or leather), and power mirrors. There are remote doors, second sliding doors on vans, and a fifth door on extended cab pickups! Don't forget tilt steering wheel and cruise control. What about dual airbags and side airbags with the on and off switches for the safety of your children, and antilock brakes? Do you want the integrated child seat? And for traveling, wouldn't it be nice to have the electronic navigation system to guide you to your destination or to retrieve your e-mail while on the road? Yes, car computers are here.

What kind of sound system do you want, cassette or CD player? And of course everybody must have a cellular phone these days (though recent studies are showing an increase of auto accidents due to cellular phones). There's also a rear window defroster, and the list goes on and on and on. And that's just the inside!

Consider your options.

Decisions, decisions, decisions— what's a consumer to do?

On the outside, you can get spoilers, bedliners, mud flaps, pin stripes, sunroofs, removable hard tops and T-tops, tinted windows, and much more! Some of these options will be standard (the options or option package that comes with a vehicle at no extra charge), but some will cost extra depending on the particular model and series you buy and what exactly it is you want. And there's the trim package (SE, SSE, XE, GXE, Deluxe, etc.) and the wheels (sport, rally, alloy, etc.). What color do you prefer? There are only 500 zillion colors and shades!

Used

Of course, if you are buying preowned, the choices you have to make are much simpler. You take what you get. However, that's not to say that you can't have aftermarket products installed. Aftermarket products are options listed above such as pin-stripes, tinted windows, sunroofs, radio systems, and other options that can be added to a new or used automobile once you've purchased it. If you buy from a dealership, these changes are made in the service department or body shop, or are subcontracted out to a reputable company with whom the dealer has developed an honorable and trustworthy working relationship.

If you buy from Joe's Used Car Lot, that's a different story. You will have to find someone yourself to do the work unless Joe can point you in the right direction. Here's a thought though; Joe's someone probably pays him a nice little commission under the table for the referral, thus costing you more money. Make sure that the company you choose or the company you are referred to is known for quality work and that they are reputable. You want to do business with someone who will stand behind his or her work and who will still be in operation

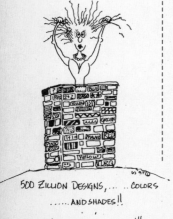

500 ZILLION DESIGNS, ...COLORS
...... AND SHADES !!

WHAT'S A WOMAN TO DO !!!

six months down the road. Also, compare pricing. You'll be surprised at the range in prices quoted!

Factory

If your plan is to order a vehicle from the factory, the decisions can become extremely overwhelming. Pick up as many product brochures on the particular model that you want (these are available to customers on display racks in dealership showrooms) and study the brochures until you think your brains are gonna explode! The more product knowledge you can grasp, the better prepared you will be. For as I continue to expose the ways of the auto industry, you will realize just how much there is to consider and how many choices there are to make. If you have questions (no matter how many), ask them! The only dumb question is the one you didn't ask!

If you are ordering a vehicle and you plan on trading one in, make sure you get in writing that you have the right to a second trade-in appraisal from a different dealer. Many times when a customer trades their car in on an ordered unit, the dealer will show $$$ amount for the trade at time of order. But when the new car finally arrives from the factory, the dealer will allow much less for the trade, claiming that the trade-in value dropped tremendously. Protect yourself. Make sure you get that second appraisal clause in writing and signed by the dealer at time of order or you will lose money!

Trade

Do you have a trade-in and if so, what is it really worth? (Not to you, but to the dealer.)

Is your trade-in running smoothly and in good operating condition? Do all the power options work and are there any oil leaks or transmission problems? How's the interior? When was the last time you had your trade-in serviced? You need to know this information because you will be asked. The salesperson will want to know why you are trading. How should you answer? You will be asked all sorts of questions about your trade-in. Are the miles showing on the odometer the actual miles, has it rolled over 99,999 or are the miles unknown for some legitimate reason? If you do trade, you will be required to sign an odometer statement verifying the condition of miles.

The dealer will want to know about any body damage and if the vehicle was ever wrecked. If so, what was the extent of the damage and where was it repaired? They'll also want to know how old the tires are and how many miles are on them. Would you be better off trading in or just selling outright? You need to know what your trade is worth before showing it to a dealer. There are several ways of obtaining this information. You can call any auto license office or bank loan department, or you can visit your local library or bookstore. They should have a number of consumers' automotive guide books. There are also used car pricing services available to consumers' for a fee. Most of the automotive clubs will also have new and used car services available to their members for a fee.

If you're fortunate enough to have access to the Internet, go sight-seeing across the Web. There's a cyber-world full of automotive information right at your fingertips. Some of it will be free and some of it won't be free depending on what exactly you're looking for or need. Regardless, though, you should be able to get a trade-in value for free. Just type in www.auto.com or some other variation of the words automotive, automobile, or car in the designated field and watch as the magical kingdom of automotive cyberspace appears before your very eyes.

Stick to your guns!

Whichever approach you choose, you will need to know the make, year, model, equipment, miles, and the condition of your vehicle. My best advice to you on this particular matter is to take it to a couple of used car lots and ask for an appraisal, preferably somewhere you know you won't be trading. Get the current wholesale value as well as the current suggested resale value. (Auto values change monthly. That's why I said to get the current values.) Tell them you want to sell your car but you don't have a clue as to what it's worth. Most likely, they will be glad to assist you, but be prepared for the turnaround—a major attempt to sell you one out of their inventory!

Thank them for their interest but politely tell them you don't need another car and stick to your guns.

I strongly suggest this because it is my opinion that there is no way to know the true value of a used automobile without actually seeing it and driving it first. There could be ten identical cars lined up side by side—same make, model, year, equipment, etc.—but each one having a different value because of the physical condition inside and outside, the component and mechanical condition, and the mileage of each. My point: no two used automobiles are identical, so how can they have identical values?

Internet

As I just mentioned, one can easily get a trade-in value from the Internet, but there is so much more information (on both new and used automobiles) readily available to anyone who is willing to spend a little time browsing.

There are new Web sites popping up daily. You can view the newest automotive lines and get their current pricing. You can find out information on the latest

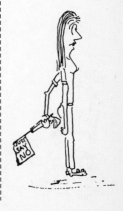

rebates, special financing, and lease programs being offered. There are reports on the latest automotive technology and safety features. If you want to inquire about automotive insurance, that's available as well, along with free quotes. And speaking of free quotes, finance and lease payments can be figured.

Manufacturers, dealerships, brokers, agents, financing and leasing companies, and buyer and leasing car services all participate in the Internet world hoping to boost sales and increase their profit. Granted, the Internet is a wonderful place to gather information, but be leery of false advertising and deals too good to be true. There is no guaranteed protection if you happen to fall victim. The legal rights of consumers are not yet set in stone and there are many kinks that must be worked out. If something were to go wrong, you're X#*0 out of luck.

One of my family members lost $2,500 by purchasing a new computer thru the Internet. The company required payment in full before they would ship out the computer, so he mailed them a check for the total amount due. He was supposed to receive the computer within a few days, but a few days turned into a few weeks, and then a few months. Unfortunately, the computer was never shipped, and the check had already cleared the bank before he found out the company had filed bankruptcy and completely shut down. He had no recourse and no way of recovering his $2,500. What a hard lesson to learn! Use the Internet as a research tool, but I would try to avoid major on-line purchases as much as possible. Fraudulent transactions are hard to detect until it's too late. On-line buying can be risky business!

MEET AND GREET ..... YOU ARE BEING "SIZED UP" !
(WHAT IS YOUR PRICE RANGE ??...)

The Meet and Greet: Prequalifying

If salespeople are trained properly and are experienced, no matter where you go to buy they will walk you through what's called the Meet and Greet and they will prequalify you. This helps them to better assist you in fulfilling your automotive needs.

Prequalifying should begin right up front when asking your name and where you live. If a salesperson tries to put you in an automobile right away, without prequalifying you, chances are he's the *new kid on the block* or the new recruit. Slow him down! You could end up buying what's simply not affordable for your budget. The automotive insurance that's required by law could also be well out of your range, or you could be pressured into buying something that you just aren't happy with. I'm not saying that every new salesperson would do this, but more often than not this happens. That's why prequalification is so crucial and by you having this foresight and taking control, you can come out smelling like the rose that you are.

When I was in sales, I used to meet my customers on the lot, introduce myself, and get their name. I would proceed to find out just a few facts like where they were from and what brought them to our dealership. After a little small talk, I would invite them into my office to find out how I could help them and discuss their needs. I would begin to prequalify them. If the customers were serious buyers they would usually follow me inside. At that point I would offer a cup of coffee or something cold to drink, and I always kept a container full of goodies for the little kids (big kids, too).

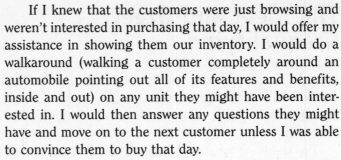

Do not mention leasing up front because you want to get that BEST NO-TRADE PURCHASE PRICE first.

If I knew that the customers were just browsing and weren't interested in purchasing that day, I would offer my assistance in showing them our inventory. I would do a walkaround (walking a customer completely around an automobile pointing out all of its features and benefits, inside and out) on any unit they might have been interested in. I would then answer any questions they might have and move on to the next customer unless I was able to convince them to buy that day.

When you are shopping for a new ride and the sales representative assisting you isn't asking the right kind of questions, or you don't feel comfortable with what's taking place, then take the wheel. Before test driving any units, ask the sales rep if you could go inside to discuss your needs first.

Tell them what you're looking for, approximately what your price range is, and only if payments are a major determining factor would you ever mention financing at this point! If that's the case, then firmly specify what that monthly payment needs to be without any credit insurance and extended warranty! (They will assume that you want the extras and will attempt to force it on you even when you tell them no.) This will help the sales team stay focused on your price range. Know how much you have for a down payment and at this point, absolutely do not mention any trade if you have one because you want to get their rock bottom sale price on a straight out purchase first. The same goes for leasing.

This way they can't jack you around on the sale price, your trade-in allowance, or the lease should you choose to go that route. Only after you've gotten their absolute best no-trade price do you throw them the loop. The loop is your trade-in. And of course you already know what your trade in is worth, right? (You better know!)

Believe me, all of this will not only save you time but most importantly, save you money! The sales team could spend a whole day showing you different makes and styles of all prices trying to guess what you want and need. But with your guidance and steadfast determination, they will know your limits right up front, and the odds of landing you in the right vehicle are increased tremendously. Another thing: "You'd better shop around!"

Do not settle for the first thing that catches your eye. Check out all of your options. You might find four or five vehicles you like at several different locations. If so, make each sales force go to the bargaining table for you and whatever you do, DO NOT EVER bite at their first offer.

Negotiate that price! Make them mark it down. It's their job, but more importantly it's your call. Don't forget—get a straight out purchase price first then bring in the trade! Once you feel you have the dealer's best price (written down by the salesperson on their purchase order—this is very important), ask for a copy, thank them and leave. They will not want to give up these figures because they know as soon as they have, more than likely you'll head straight to another dealership to shop and compare their price.

When customers won't commit to buying, they are usually T.O.'d (turned over) to a closer. A closer is someone whose primary job is to close that sale, convince that customer to buy before leaving the lot. Don't let yourself be pressured into buying on the spot no matter what story they conjure up! If the price is good today, it will be good tomorrow! Once you've collected all of your different price offers, go home and review them. Only then will you truly be able to compare prices and save money.

If you have a trustworthy friend in the automobile business who works in sales, take advantage of that situ-

"You'd better shop around!"

DO NOT EVER bite at their first offer.

Shopping? Imagine that. Who-ever heard of such a thing?

Knowledge is power. You should know what you want, understand how to get it (have a plan), and, finally, GO AFTER IT!

By spot delivering, the dealer can easily claim problems. MAYBE THEY EXIST – MAYBE THEY DON'T!

ation and ask him or her to help you, but don't lose control! Keep your guard up. Even though you are no stranger to this person, your friend's (or whoever it is) job is still to make as much profit as possible, as much as you will allow. Recognize when you are being pre-qualified and recall the steps and facts you now have.

And speaking of buying on the spot, if you are a finance customer, and if they know you are still on the hunt, the sales force will attempt to spot deliver you. Spot delivery is when the dealer convinces a customer to drive home in their new vehicle before receiving an actual approval for a loan, and after signing all the necessary forms including a finance contract.

BAD IDEA! Don't do it. Not only is it a major ploy to end your search for that "best deal" and keep you in their merchandise, but it's an easy way to ask for more profit without you knowing. Plus, all sorts of things could backfire. You'll drive their unit home. A day later, you will receive a phone call from them asking you to come back in and resign some more papers because supposedly there is a problem. Maybe there is and maybe there isn't. You'll be told that the bank they ran your loan through did not approve it, but they did get you approved elsewhere. When you get to the dealership, you'll find that the interest rate has gone up and the payments have gone up also. Or they might tell you that the bank wants a larger down payment (again, maybe they do and maybe they don't).

Warning: Absolutely do not sign any forms whatsoever at this stage of the game unless you want your credit file pulled. No matter how long or short the forms are and no matter what creative name they call them, 99.9% of the time any form put in front of you that requires your signature will include an authorization clause to pull a credit report. The authorization clause is usually at the very bottom or on the back of the form in such tiny hard to read print that it's not noticeable.

There is a right time for everything. Only consider signing any forms *after* you have decided to purchase an automobile and *after* you have decided to finance through the dealer. Not until then!

What Kind Are You?

There are many different kinds of buyers out there. What kind are you? Do you have the right or wrong attitude? Do you know what you should and shouldn't say? Can you role-play (act) to get what you want? There is a script for you and your performance will affect the final scene. You could come home with or without that Emmy award. How you communicate with a sales team could save you a ton of money or could cost you dearly.

The Know-It-All

If indeed you are an experienced buyer, don't be a know-it-all! If you go shopping with the attitude that you know everything about everything, it's only going to hurt you. First of all, as a rule in life nobody in this world knows everything. Secondly, you can never stop learning. Finally, nobody likes a know-it-all. Even if you have studied your situation thoroughly and know exactly what you want, what you can and can't afford, and how you are going to accomplish your goal, there might be circumstances that could improve your overall picture, no matter how good or how bad it is. Certain factors change from day to day such as dealer and customer rebates. They directly affect discounts offered. The prime rate directly

Dealers attempt to play "Sherlock Holmes" by investigating your credit history without your knowledge.

NOBODY LIKES A KNOW-IT-ALL!

affects interest rates, incentives from the factory, and special finance and lease programs. If you are unwilling to at least listen to what the dealer has to say, you could possibly cut your own throat. Oh, did I mention—nobody likes a know-it-all?

The Know-Nothing

DUH!

Oh dear! Catch me, I'm going to faint. Please read my book before venturing out! Remember school finals? If you didn't study (and the teacher somehow always knew), you were dead. It's like the cat and the mouse. The salesperson is the cat and the know-nothing customer is the mouse. The cat will sniff you out immediately and will proceed to claim you as his next victim. You'll end up paying much more than necessary. Again, it's not what you know, but what you don't know that gets you in trouble.

The How-Much-a-Month

Don't croak and choke before you drive!

The only time you should ever inform the dealer of your desired payment (without insurance and extended warranty) is if and only if it is a do-or-die situation. At the same time, be cautious and know that many dealers try to close a sale based on your desired payment in an attempt to steer you away from the bottom dollar price. If you waltz in quoting $250 per month as your desired payment, the dealer will milk it for all it's worth and assume that you don't care what price or method of payment it is, so long as that payment is $250 per month. Warning: You could be cheating yourself out of lots of money and a fancier, better-equipped ride. Let's say that you have quoted your desired payment. The dealer will choose the cheapest unit possible to reach your goal. However, the payment could be loaded up with life and accidental

health insurance and extended warranty, or at least as much of that stuff as $250 will hold for 100 months. (They will pretend to forget what you said about the extras and try to sell you on the fact that your payment will be totally protected!)

These extras added to your payment are not mandatory. Without all that protection, your payment could be as low as $190 per month. That's a savings of $60 per month. Make sure they aren't selling you a lease. Be sure to buy the most vehicle possible for your money first. In other words, get your base payment (without all the extras jokingly known as *laha, croak, and choke*), then discuss insurance and extended warranty and leasing later on in the finance office with the finance manager.

Ms. ...... How Much A month ??

Ms. Be-Careful-My-Boyfriend-Is-Here

If you go into a dealership or a used car lot with a threatening and defensive attitude, your actions will only create friction between you and the sales team (sales person and sales manager). They will be less willing to assist you and chances are they will try even harder to make more profit on you than the customer with a good attitude. No sales person wants to be intimidated by the bully you've brought along. That's exactly how your boyfriend will be perceived, as a bully! LEAVE HIM AT HOME UNLESS YOU BOTH CAN SHOP WITH THE RIGHT ATTITUDE.

My boyfriend's back and there's gonna be trouble? I don't think so!

Ms. This-Is-My-Father

If your father is with you more than likely you will be shown more respect than a woman who shows up alone. Or I should say your father would be shown more respect. The dealer will view you (with your father) as a serious

AND IN THE RIGHT-HAND CORNER WE HAVE . . .

buyer and won't want to agitate the situation in any way. The sales force will try to close your deal that day because from their perspective, right or wrong, they will see your father as the decision-maker. Keep in mind, your father is there to help, and there is no need for an attack so leave the dukes at home. Be cordial and you just might save some money. If you attack, you're asking for it.

The Best-of-Everything

Some people think they have to have the very best, most expensive, fanciest paint job, deluxe trim package, and of course, the latest in technology. This is okay if you have a money tree growing in your back yard and you can truly afford this kind of sumptuous living. But is it sensible? Are you trying to keep up with the Joneses or is this what you really need and can afford? Don't forget that expensive auto insurance goes right along with an expensive ride. One can easily get caught up in the flashy neon lights if you're not careful. Just how much of that green foliage are you willing to pick from your trees? The dealer will be celebrating. That you can count on!

The How-Will-I-Look-in-It

I do declare Ms. Susan . . . what am I gonna do with you? Would you please stop worrying about how you're going to look in your new ride and concentrate on your needs, your financial situation, and dependability! If money is an object, your options are narrowed. If money isn't an object, the sky is the limit. Just remember to buy what you want as long as it's within your means; not what someone

> If you've got the money, they've definitely got the time. And they'll go honky-tonkin'—ALL THE WAY TO THE BANK!

> I'm too sexy for my ___, too sexy for my ___, I'm too sexy . . .

TOO SEXY FOR MY ___ , TOO SEXY FOR MY ~~~ I'M TOO SEXY!

else thinks you should buy. You have to live with your purchase, not them.

The Let's-Get-This-Over-With

One of the biggest mistakes a potential buyer can make is to rush into an automotive purchase. Getting all nervous and bent out of shape will only hurt you. You must take your time and do some thought processing. Take advantage of the prequalification stage and think everything through. Be sure that everyone involved knows and understands your situation. Let the sales person show you around but do not jump into the first set of wheels that comes along! Make sure you test drive several units, gather all of your information on each one, including their best no-trade price, and then study all of your options—at home. You don't want buyer's remorse (bitter regret) later on, do you?

Unbreak my heart, please!

REINFORCE-MENT: No matter what kind of buyer you are or who you are buying from (even if it's your best friend), make sure you test drive each and every unit you are considering before purchasing. And if you're considering a used automobile, always go down the Used Car Checklist (provided in Chapter 4).

....Do NOT...JUMP INTO THE FIRST SET OF WHEELS THAT COME ALONG !!!

CHAPTER 3

The Vehicle:
Advantages and Disadvantages

I n this chapter, I'll analyze the different classifications of vehicles and point out some of the advantages and disadvantages of each. Much of this information is basic knowledge and a lot of common sense, but nonetheless, it is still important enough to review. There just might be one little factor you haven't considered that could possibly change your final destination.

New

This one is pretty much self-explanatory: an automobile fresh off the assembly line that has been delivered to a dealership. Technically, this particular automobile still has the Certificate of Origin (original papers straight from the factory) and has never been sold or transferred to anyone but the new auto dealer. It will have a full factory warranty with the amount of time and miles covered under the warranty varying among different manufacturers.

Advantages

First ownership: having the peace of mind and satisfaction of knowing that you're not inheriting someone else's problems. Bumper-to-bumper factory war-

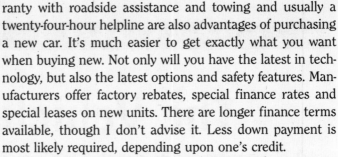

To get a copy of your state's law, apply to the state attorney general's office where you live. Lemon laws may vary from state to state.

ranty with roadside assistance and towing and usually a twenty-four-hour helpline are also advantages of purchasing a new car. It's much easier to get exactly what you want when buying new. Not only will you have the latest in technology, but also the latest options and safety features. Manufacturers offer factory rebates, special finance rates and special leases on new units. There are longer finance terms available, though I don't advise it. Less down payment is most likely required, depending upon one's credit.

Consumers are protected by the lemon laws, and may take legal steps towards arbitration. If a consumer purchases a vehicle that turns out to be a lemon and there have been repeated attempts to repair the problem with no success, and it is determined that the problem cannot be resolved, then the consumer has the right to arbitration. The dispute is settled and a replacement vehicle of equal value is usually the ending result.

Disadvantages

Identical models can be found at different locations. This creates the need to shop from dealer to dealer, which not only takes a lot more time, but also marches you right into the dealer price battle zone. Higher initial costs, higher insurance costs, and higher payments go right along with a new purchase. If one pays cash, interest that would normally be earned on invested money is lost. Also, a new vehicle will have a high depreciation immediately.

Demo

Short for demonstrator, this is a new vehicle that has been put into demo service and driven by a dealer or dealer employee (usually as a job benefit as well as a systematic means and very cost-efficient way to promote the product line). Once a demo reaches a certain mileage, it is taken out of demo service and parked back on the lot with the remaining inventory to sell. Demos are always available to you for purchase whether they are currently in demo service or not.

Advantages

You can expect greater savings, especially at the end of the year closeout sales. Dealers are anxious to get rid of any leftover inventory in order to bring in the new year models. (It's out with the old, in with the new!) In most cases, any existing problems with a demo, whether it is mechanical or other, will have already been taken care of by the service department or body shop. New finance and lease programs, rebates, and special interest rates apply to new demos. Remainder of factory warranty applies. So long as demos have been in service (in use) less than twelve months or 12,000 miles, they qualify for new extended warranty. Time and mileage may vary depending on the manufacturer and the extended warranty company.

You can expect greater savings, especially at the end of the year closeout sales.

Disadvantages

There could possibly be some interior and exterior damages such as cigarette burns (most dealerships will not allow employees to smoke in their demos), wear to the seats and panels, or dings and scratches to the body and paint. Also, when a new unit is placed into demo service, the factory warranty goes into effect that day. This is called the in-service date. Consequently, when a demo is sold, the factory warranty begins on the in-service date, not the purchase date. The new owner loses all of the time period that has passed and all mileage that has been driven.

Program/Executive

These two classifications are very similar in that both are pre-owned and sold to dealers and wholesalers through automotive auctions. Program units are usually previously owned by rental companies such as Hertz and Avis, or previously owned by companies that operate a fleet (a group of automobiles) for their business. When rental units reach a certain mileage (the mileage will vary depending on the individual company policy), they are pulled off of rental service and resold through auto auctions, unless the rental company has its own used car lot. In that case, they are sold there. New units replace the used ones.

Program units can also be previously owned and leased through independent leasing companies or the manufacturers, or even dealerships if they have an in-house lease program. When a lease has ended and the lessee (the customer that is leasing) has downed their option to purchase the unit, it is returned to the lessor (the leasing company) and again sold either at auction or at the leasing company's own lot if they have one. Note that the mileage on a leased unit could be high based upon the leased term, (the longer the lease is, the higher the miles).

Executive units are previously owned by the automotive manufacturing companies and are driven by their management executives. You will find that the mileage on these units is very low and won't exceed much over 5,000 miles. They are sold through factory-sponsored auctions at which only legitimate dealership representatives are allowed. And of course, executives get their new set of wheels!

Program units can also be previously owned and leased through independent leasing companies or the manufacturers, or even dealerships if they have an in-house lease program.

Advantages

This is a great way to buy an almost new vehicle and save some major bucks. On program units, the remainder of the factory warranty is transferable to the second owner, usually for a minimal fee. The dealer should inform you of this amount. On program and executive units, if your purchase date falls within twelve months and 12,000 miles of the original in-service date, you have the option to buy a new car extended warranty. Once again, time and mileage allowances may vary depending on the manufacturer and the extended warranty company.

Been there—
done that—
not good!

Disadvantages

Even though you are saving money, a program/executive unit is still a used automobile. There could possibly be some hidden conditions resulting from a wreck, such as leaks and cheap paint jobs, that require further investment down the road. These types of problems would not be covered under your warranty. The dealer might or might not have known about any existing problems when the purchasing transaction took place, but as you've been warned, that is a chance you take when buying used merchandise. Been there—done that—not good!

Used

Used is used, (any preowned, prerented, or preleased unit). This could include one that's six months old or twenty years old. Anything much older would fall into the antique category and that is not what this book is about. Different topic/different author.

Advantages

A used automobile obviously costs less than a new one of the same make and model and the insurance is also cheaper. Like the new, the used market is huge and competitive, thus making it easier to find good quality as well as affordable transportation; that is, if you're shopping in reputable territory! Extended warranties are available on some used inventory depending on—guess what? Right! Age and mileage! There are now many finance programs available on used inventory as an alternative to those who have tried to buy a new vehicle and can't due to past credit problems.

Disadvantages

Did you get what you paid for? Need I say more? By taking the chance of inheriting a nightmare on wheels, your initial purchase could possibly be just the beginning of a long nickel-and-dime battle. Lenders are much more stringent on the amount of money they will loan on used inventory, and terms (number of payments) are generally shorter. Limited or no warranty at all is dependent on, once again, age and miles. Many older models do not meet the legal standards and requirements of current law, therefore, won't pass inspection, which brings me to the newest safety features. Many used units will not have these features, nor will they have the latest technology and options.

One more classification of used auto sales is the *certified* used car. They're mostly top-quality reconditioned trade-ins or auction units that can range in age and have met an extensive 100-plus point inspection either by the dealer service department or by the manufacturer. Since they meet the standard requirements, they're usually sold with some type of warranty coverage. The amount of warranty coverage is up to each individual dealer/manufacturer. The particulars on certified used car programs may vary from franchise to franchise. Ask your dealer for details. In regard to the lemon law, it also applies to some used automobiles.

I hope this chapter has been beneficial by giving you a more clearly defined view of the market. Of course, not all advantages and disadvantages are listed—that could go on and on!

Attention Automotive Shoppers: Fasten you seatbelts and put the pedal to the metal. Prepare to drive through the chancy world of used cars!

Used Cars and Used Car Lots

Most everyone has a story. Maybe they swear by it. Maybe they swear at it. One thing is for sure, there's no shortage of places to find used cars. But whom do you trust? Talk to twenty people, you'll get twenty different stories. Some good, some bad, and some downright unbelievable. The most important person in a purchase will always remain you.

You are the one that has to decide if you're knowledgeable enough to choose a sound used automobile. If not, then stick with the new ones. If for some reason you have to buy used, there are plenty of things you can do to tip the odds in favor of getting both a good deal and good quality.

Dealership/Auction

A great place to look for a used vehicle is the new car dealership. They keep the best trade-ins for their customers. The older models or the real junkers are taken to the auction or sold to wholesale dealers. A used car manager doesn't have time to tinker with anything that's not cream of the crop, nor does he have a place for them on his lot. He has to keep good quality units in his used car inventory. If the number gets low, he will go to the auto auction and buy more. (This is not a public auction, but one where only licensed

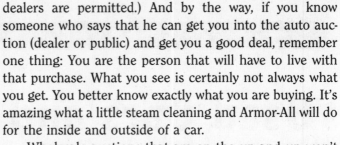

You are the one that has to decide if you're knowledge-able enough to choose a sound used automobile.

Shines up real good, and just look at them wheels sparkle. Ya know what I mean, Vern?

dealers are permitted.) And by the way, if you know someone who says that he can get you into the auto auc-tion (dealer or public) and get you a good deal, remember one thing: You are the person that will have to live with that purchase. What you see is certainly not always what you get. You better know exactly what you are buying. It's amazing what a little steam cleaning and Armor-All will do for the inside and outside of a car.

Wholesale auctions that are on the up and up won't let just anyone in. Find out exactly how much this friend of yours is going to make for lending his name to the deal, and ask if he is willing to help you pay for needed repairs if it turns out you bought an unveiled nightmare.

Sure, there's no dickering at auctions and you get the inside track, but it's an avenue that I personally would steer clear of unless I knew how I could unload a bad purchase without losing my shirt. You're not sup-posed to be there in the first place, so whom can you turn to? Even a dealer can get stung at an auction, but he will have the resources to repair his bad purchase and can afford to make it saleable. He will have more money in his purchase than originally planned but will not get stuck with it. The buyers that represent him have their jobs riding on their selections; too many bad selections and they are history! The only one you can turn to is standing in front of the mirror every morning staring right back.

Overall, large dealers will have a wide range of reliable used vehicles. They may own several types of used car lots. One might be all top of the line cream puff stuff. They might have lesser quality units at a lot further down the street. Over a couple of blocks under a different name they might have a buy-here pay-here lot, which has the less desirable units for customers with less than desirable credit who absolutely cannot get financed. The smart dealers are in the auto business for the long haul and will do most anything to get your business.

Superstore

The name speaks for itself. In fact, the superstore lots with their high-quality inventories are so huge that customers have the option of picking out the vehicle of their choice from computer monitors while sitting in the comforts of a fancy office. Some of the superstores even have restaurants and playrooms for the little tots. These added conveniences definitely cut down on the *Be-Backs*. (Be-Backs are those customers who almost buy a car, but for one reason or another, do not and leave the dealership saying that they will be back. Usually, Be-Backs will not return).

Superstores are mostly chain stores such as Auto-Nation, USA, CarMax, Car America, and SmartCars, all of which will soon be nationwide. There are some independent superstores. They all offer no-haggle pricing on purchased units and no-haggle pricing on trade-ins (wholesale value). They have finance departments with all the trimmings (aftermarket products, insurance, and extended warranties) and service departments. Though their inventories are extremely plentiful and they offer shopping in comfort and convenience, superstores are not exactly famous for having the lowest prices.

SHINES UNDERNEATH HOOD .... REAL GOOD .... AND JUST LOOK AT THE WHEELS SPARKLE!

> You buy their special of the day and they take the money and run.

YOU BUY THEIR "SPECIAL OF THE DAY."

Independent Lots

The independent used car lot comes in all shapes and sizes. Some of the biggest you might be hard pressed to distinguish from a new car dealership. They will have showrooms, service departments, parts departments, and occasionally you'll find one with a body shop. They have finance departments just as sophisticated as the new car dealerships that offer credit insurance and extended warranties. They do a super job and are a good source for quality used automobiles.

Then there are some really nice used lots that aren't so big and sophisticated. They try to find quality merchandise and don't knowingly sell a bad unit. Consider them as a good source. There won't be as many *cherries* to pick from most likely, but you might be surprised. The independents tend to develop a reputation for selling a certain type in a given price range. You can tell a great deal about a used car dealer in a drive-by of the lot to see what kind of inventory is on display. They won't have an on-site service department but will have mechanics they use for repairs needed to make a vehicle saleable, such as an independent garage. But make no mistake, a used auto dealer won't do any major repairs, only enough to make units saleable.

All used auto dealers, no matter how large or small, are required by law to use what is called a Federal Buyers Guide. This is a sticker form that is placed on the window of any used automobile being sold. It simply states the condition of sale of the vehicle: As-Is No Warranty, 3 months/3,000-mile limited warranty on engine, transmission, and drive axle, remainder of factory warranty, etc. The type of war-

ranty, if any, is up to the dealer. He is not required to provide any other than the remaining factory warranties that
automatically come with the unit. The buyers guide should
always be used. If you are looking at a used car on a lot
and do not see the sticker, ask where it is. The caution flag
should go up. Shady dealer?

I'm sure you've seen the specials on TV about shady
dealers. Yes, they're definitely out there and they tend to
be low-budget operations that aren't around very long.
Sometimes it seems as if the disappearing act is by design.

You can often tell by their lot locations; many are in
low-rent districts. They are there to swindle money from
unsuspecting individuals who feel they have no choice but
to buy from these characters due to credit difficulties
and/or little money.

Take heed:
You do have
a choice!

Buy-Here Pay-Here Lots

The buy-here pay-here lots can be beneficial if you are
stuck between a rock and a hard place. Even dealerships
can have this option available. In today's auto world, there
are secondary finance sources specifically designed for
those who have had past credit problems but are now
trying to get re-established.

The problem with buy-here pay-here programs is that
you will pay astronomical prices and astronomical
interest rates. But if you're walking and can't get
financed anywhere else, what do you do? If you have to
pay a high dollar to get back on track, then maybe it's
worth it. That is another decision you have to make.
The vehicles at a buy-here pay-here lot are not of
the best quality, but they are transportation for
those who have no alternative. And there are

"SHADY DEALERS" TAKE THE MONEY AND RUN...

If you've been striking out and you feel like there's no hope, don't give up. Know that there is a silver lining behind every troubled sky, but you have to reach high above the clouds to find it. Only then will you find brighter days ahead.

exceptions. Shop only at establishments who have a reputation for fairness and honesty. Just don't miss a payment! They will take the car back in a flash!

Be wary if a lot claims they can help you rebuild your credit. There is only one way, and that is to report your payment record to the credit bureau. If they don't report your good payment record, then that good performance will do nothing to change your bad credit history. Ask them if they report. If they say yes, then what do you have to lose by checking with the bureau they supposedly report to? All it takes is a phone call. It will also give you an indication of whether the dealer is being honest or not. If he doesn't tell you the truth about credit reporting, do you think you should buy from him? Also, make sure that the credit bureau is a common source for credit information such as Trans Union, Equifax, and CBA. It won't do any good to have your credit record sitting at XYZ Credit Bureau if nobody ever checks it!

With Your Eyes Wide Open, and Your Ears, and Your Nose, and Your . . .

Ask a simple question and you may not get a simple answer. Getting the truth from a car dealer is sometimes virtually impossible, especially if the automobile you're interested in has a bad rap. Obviously, the dealer wants to make a sale and anything that might hinder that sale will not be revealed unless you happened to see it, find out about it, or ask specific questions. Even then it's hard to get the truth. As far as the dealer is concerned, every unit on his lot is a jewel.

They've all been inspected top to bottom, inside and out, blah, blah, blah. I've already told you that the best way to protect yourself when buying a used car is to hire a reliable and trustworthy mechanic and have it checked out extensively. The cost will vary depending on where you live but if you're going to invest thousands of dollars, isn't it worth the extra bucks to make the right decision? Don't trust scorpions. Their sting hurts.

If you can't afford to hire a mechanic, there are some things you can check for yourself. With the help of my friend Ben, who is a professional mechanic and shop owner, we put together an easy-to-follow checklist for evaluating the condition of any automobile you might be considering. Some are fairly basic and some are more in-depth. Evaluating a used car has to be more than jumping in for a quick test drive down the road. Whatever you do, tune in all your senses, then proceed.

SEE
HEAR
SMELL
TOUCH

Used Car Checklist

Air Conditioner Make sure the air works. Turn the air on to its coldest temperature setting. Have someone inside of the vehicle turning the air on and off while you stand outside listening under the hood. You should hear it clicking on and off. If the air isn't cold maybe the refrigerant level is low. If that's not the problem, maybe the compressor is going out. This is a very expensive item to replace.

Battery Check the battery for any corrosion around the cables and check for cracking or swelling of the battery casing. If any of these are visible, the battery needs to be replaced. It's no biggy, but why should you pay for it?

Do a personal inspection.

Belts Look at the inside of the belts that face the pulleys, the part that is hard to see. Check for dryness and cracking. They may need to be replaced.

Brakes When you apply the brakes listen for grinding, squeaking noises, or vibration in the steering wheel. This could indicate some brake problems such as worn out brake pads. If the emergency brake comes all the way up and does not hold the automobile like it should, the rear brakes could be out of adjustment or worn out.

Brake Fluid Leakage Look underneath the car like you're trying to look at the inside of the tire. Now look on the backside of the brake backing plate for wetness. Oily wetness on the inside of either tire or wheel would indicate brake fluid leakage. Check the brake fluid level. If it's low, there is probably a problem with the brakes.

Carburetor Mostly found on older automobiles, and because of their many parts, they are prone to be problematic. Newer automobiles are fuel-injected. The carburetor mixes fuel and air to produce an explosive vapor. Check for wetness (fuel leakage) on top of the motor at the base of the carburetor.

Catalytic Converter The catalytic converter is a pollution control device on the tail pipe. If the car is shaking, missing, or hard to keep running, or if the exhaust smells like rotten eggs, there is probably a catalytic converter problem. If the exhaust smells really strong like raw gas and burns your eyes, it's probably some other emission problem. One or more of the sensors may not be working properly.

Clipping This is when the front of one car is welded to the back of another car, usually from wrecked or stolen units. Also known as chopping, thus the term *chop shops*. Look for welding seams underneath the front of the front seat or front of the back seat. Also look for new undercoating. Check inside the trunk for a color match. If you think you've come across a clipped unit, don't buy it!

Clutch (standard transmission) If a clutch is bad, gears will slip. Accelerate the automobile increasing the speed and changing gears. If the gears slip, the motor will be revving and you won't be going anywhere.

Components Check all of the components on the vehicle and make sure every single button and switch is working, including the cigarette lighter. If the windows are manual, make sure they roll up and down. Anything that doesn't work properly can be a tool to chisel that price down.

Cooling System The cooling system keeps the engine from overheating and also from freezing. The fluid used in this system is called coolant, and antifreeze is added to the coolant. Before you start up the car, pull the radiator cap off while it's cold. Do not open it while it's hot! You could be seriously burned. Look to see if the liquid is brownish orange or rusty in color. If it is, there is a leak in the system and air is causing oxidation. The metals from the cooling system are oxidizing, turning the fluids to a watery rusty color. The cooling system is a closed liquid system and when air gets in, it starts to run low. This can lead to some major engine problems. The rusty liquid is usually a good indication of poor maintenance by the previous owner. They probably poured water into the radiator on a regular basis. Again, possible major engine problems.

Crank Shaft If you hear taps and knocks when you crank up the engine, step on the gas pedal and listen to see if the noises quiet down. If, however, as the engine idles again you hear the tapping and knocking, there is probably a crankshaft problem.

CV Joints Constant velocity joints are on the front of front-wheel drive vehicles as part of the drive axle. They allow the wheels to turn. Find a large parking lot to test drive in. Start out by cutting the wheel all the way to the left and drive counterclockwise in as tight a circle as you can at about ten miles per hour. Listen for a clicking noise in the front. Then turn the wheel all the way to the right doing the same thing, listening for the clicking noise. If noises are present, the CV joints could be bad, which would mean the front axles would need to be replaced.

There is a protective rubber boot about 4–6 inches long that looks like a funnel covering the CV joints. If they break they are rather expensive to replace. The boots crack open, grease slings out, and they get dry. Dirt, water, and rocks get up inside and grind up the CV joints. Sometimes you can get away with putting new boots on, but if the clicking continues or returns, you'll have to replace the joints.

Doors Many things can be determined by the doors. Open up the doors and check the doorjambs (the inside of the doors—the part you don't see when the door is shut). If the car has been repainted, often the doorjambs won't get painted. Compare the shades of color. Grab the door and move it up and down to check the strength of door hinges. Check to see if doors open and close properly. Weak hinges and hard to open and close doors may indicate that the vehicle was involved in an accident. Check door handles for missing parts or to see if they are loose from having to slam the door. Check the door panels for the same looseness.

Electrical System Check all of the lights: headlights, parking lights, interior lights, hazard lights, and brake lights. Also check turning signals and anything else related to the electrical system such as wipers, sound system, power windows, power door locks, power seats, etc. Check the bulbs, fuses, and casings. Make sure they are all good and not broken. If any are not working properly or broken, ask for them to be replaced. There could be another underlying problem. Electrical system repairs are not cheap and you certainly don't want to buy a *fire waiting to happen!*

Emergency Brake You should not be able to drive off with the emergency brake on. If you can, the cable is probably loose or broken and needs to be tightened or replaced. Also, if the emergency brake comes all the way up and doesn't hold the car like it should, the rear brakes are possibly out of adjustment or worn out.

Empty Containers If buying from an individual, look for empty containers of oil, water, antifreeze, etc. in the floorboard or in the trunk of the vehicle. Major red flags should go up if any are found. Empty containers are signs of problems. Dealers will usually remove any and all evidence before putting the car out on the lot.

> You should not be able to drive off with the emergency brake on.

> If buying from an individual, look for empty containers of oil, water, antifreeze, etc. in the floorboard or in the trunk of the vehicle.

Engine Problems Always have a compression test run on any vehicle you are seriously considering. A compression check will usually tell all if there are internal engine problems. This will cost but is worth it, especially if the automobile is an expensive unit.

Exhaust First, check the mounting of the tailpipe. Give it a good shake and wiggle it around. If it's loose (which it shouldn't be), check for possible rust. Next, start the vehicle and after it has run for a while, take a rag in your hand and hold it over the end of the tailpipe. Make sure it has built up adequate pressure. It should go poof when you pull your hand away. Check the tailpipe for any black, sooty, or oily wetness and be leery of blue smoke that you might see. White smoke is steam and is normal.

Flood Car You can easily get ripped off on a flood car if you don't know what to look for. A flood car that has not been properly cleaned will have a moldy, musty odor. Look for water lines and rusted spots underneath the carpet and along the insides of the doors. If the car is new and on sale at an unbelievably low price, be careful. There are no spectacular deals. Six to eight months after a flood, these units will begin to pop up everywhere.

Floor Mats Again, look under floor mats and carpet for rust. This can be a major problem that is difficult if not impossible to repair.

Fluids Take the time to have the levels, color, and thickness of all the fluids checked. Refer to the owners manual if it has one or try to find one so you won't be totally in the dark. (Low fluid levels may indicate leaks and poor maintenance, which can cause serious problems). While out on a test drive, pull into a service station somewhere and have it done. It's quick, clean, and usually free. There's no need for you to get all dirty when it only takes a few minutes. Tell the person assisting you that you want a quick check of all the fluids (that's all) because you are considering buying the vehicle. You would like to know if everything looks okay or if there are possible signs of maintenance neglect. They will probably be glad to help you. Of course if you have a relative or a good friend that's a mechanic and is near by, take it to them.

Here's a fluid checklist:

Here's a fluid checklist.

- Brake Fluid
- Coolant
- Antifreeze
- Power Steering Fluid
- Oil
- Transmission Fluid
- Windshield Washer Fluid

Front-Wheel Drive The car is pulled by power that is transferred from the engine to the two front wheels. The CV joints are part of a front-wheel drive auto. Listen for the noises and clicking.

Gaskets They are the rubber seals that fit in between two parts, preventing wear or escape of fluids. Wetness probably means bad gaskets.

Hood Shocks If an automobile has hood shocks and you have to prop up the hood with something, then the hood shocks need to be replaced. This is dangerous, especially around children. The hood could fall and seriously injure someone.

Warning—
Sometimes a
mileage roll-
back unit
will slip
right
through the
cracks, no
matter how
careful you
are.

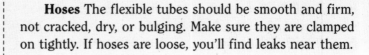

Hoses The flexible tubes should be smooth and firm, not cracked, dry, or bulging. Make sure they are clamped on tightly. If hoses are loose, you'll find leaks near them.

Liftgate and Trunk Shocks Same rules apply as with hood shocks. Bad shocks must be replaced. They can result in serious injuries.

Lighter Check to see if the lighter has been used a lot. You can tell if the previous owner was a smoker. A smoker's car tends to be more worn than a nonsmoker's car. Example: A smoker might drop a cigarette while driving and attempt to pick the cigarette up. In the process, the driver runs off the road and hits a pothole (not good for the car). Look for burn holes found on the seats, floorboard, carpet/mats, or on interior panels. A smoker's car is harder to clean and obviously will have that smoke odor. Also, check the ashtray for melted spots.

Mileage Rollback Mileage rollback is a major federal offense. If the automobile you're looking at has an analog (manual) odometer, it's easy to roll back the mileage, so you must pay close attention to this. Look at the odometer closely, especially the number farthest to the left (the number that counts). Observe carefully and look for marks, scratches, dots, etc. If you see any, rest assured that the odometer has been tampered with. Also, look at how the numbers line up. They should be perfectly straight across except for the number farthest to the right, which is the tenth/mile digit that rolls continuously. Notice the interior. Does the wear and tear of the interior reflect the mileage, especially around the driver seat? If the interior has excessive wear and the mileage is low, the odometer has probably been rolled back. Check the gas, brake, and clutch pads on the pedals. Pedal pads are good indicators of mileage. They could show the difference in a car that has 60,000 miles versus one that has 160,000 miles.

If the automobile you are considering has an electronic odometer, you can't really tell if it has been rolled back just by looking. This type of odometer is disconnected. This is something a mechanic would have to check out. However, you can still observe the wear of the interior and the wear of the pedal pads. One other safeguard you can take regardless of whether the vehicle has an analog or electronic odometer is to get the Vehicle Identification Number and run a title search through your local license office. Check the reported mileage on previous titles.

The following is a perfect example.

Jean, a good friend of mine, had bought a used car a couple of years ago. Supposedly this car had 25,000 miles on it. As time went by she began to notice little things, such as the interior which really looked too worn for a car with only 25,000 miles. About a year and a half later, Jean started having all sorts of major mechanical problems and had to get a new transmission along with several other costly repairs. After the repairs were complete she received a letter from the U.S. Supreme Court stating that her car was suspected of being part of an *odometer rollback scheme* involving three lease companies located in three different states. The courts got involved because the scheme crossed state lines. After receiving the letter, Jean realized that the value of her car had suddenly crashed through the floor and she no longer wanted it. Because of the legal implications, she couldn't trade it or sell it to anyone without getting sued, so her only option was to take it back to the dealer where she originally bought it.

If the automobile you are considering has an electronic odometer, you can't really tell if it has been rolled back just by looking.

You just never know what you are going to buy into, or should I say "roll" into?

But before she did, she took the car around to different lots and got several appraisals with the mileage it currently showed, never mentioning anything about the rollback scheme. She then took her car and the highest appraisal to the original dealer and insisted on getting that for a trade-in value. He granted Jean her wish and she unhappily drove out of the car lot that day with her very first new car. She had always bought used cars, but after what had happened she was uncomfortable with buying anything but a new one.

One month after buying her new car, she received another letter from the U.S. Supreme Court. It was a confirmation letter stating that the used car she had first bought was indeed part of that rollback scheme and that it had 50,000 more miles on it than the odometer reading reflected at time of purchase. The letter listed a phone number to call if she had any questions and wanted to follow up. Jean called the number but was told by the attorney handling the case that there were so many units involved that she would probably never see restitution. Shortly after that she received yet another letter, this time from the dealer's insurance company offering her restitution not only for her troubles, but also for her out-of-pocket expenses as well.

She took the insurance company up on their offer and the situation was finally resolved. Jean came out ahead in the long run but not everyone is so fortunate.

Motor Mount Check this one with caution. Raise the hood on the vehicle. Now sit in the driver seat and hold your foot on the brake. Be extremely careful! Put the vehicle in gear and press the gas pedal while still holding your foot to the brake. DON'T RELEASE THAT BRAKE PEDAL! If you're by yourself, look through the bottom of the hood through the windshield and watch the motor. See if it jumps or raises up any at all. It could mean the motor mount is bad or broken. Again, be careful with this one. Better yet, get someone to help you. Experiment with your own vehicle first—know what you are doing, in other words!

Muffler The muffler is attached to the tailpipe, which quiets the noise from the exhaust system. The muffler should fit tightly. Start the vehicle up and if you hear noise, chances are that the muffler is either loose, cracked, or rusted out, in which case you would need a new muffler.

Paint Always check paint for cracks, bubbles, rough places, and rust spots. Look for over-spray on trims or moldings, underneath the hood, around the tires, etc. Are there any variations in the color on different sections of the vehicle? (Example: trunk versus lower part of fender.) Here's a little tip. Take a soft refrigerator magnet and run it along the body of the automobile. This is one way of checking for putty filling in the body. These are all indicators of body damage or wrecked units.

> Always check paint for cracks, bubbles, rough places, and rust spots.

Previous Driver Question the seller/individual about the previous driver. Was it the little old lady from Pasadena that drove ever so carefully so as not to make a scratch or ding, or was it the young punk kid that rip-roared around all night racing the streets until 1:00 in the morning? Maybe it was a business consultant that traveled extensively racking up the miles. Consider the driver factor before making your final decision.

Radiator Cautiously pull the radiator cap off before you start the automobile, but only if it's cold. ***Do not open if it's***

Do not open
if it's hot!

hot! Look to see if the fluid is a brownish-orange or rusty color. This could reflect poor maintenance. Rusty color in the radiator is caused by oxidation. The metals from the cooling system are oxidizing because there is air in the system, which means there is a leak somewhere. The cooling system is a closed liquid system and when air gets in, the water level gets low, and the metal of the radiator oxidizes and causes the rusty colored water. Look for silver metal filings. That's a kind of additive that will block up leaks added by someone seeking a quick fix. Check for fin rot. Run your fingers up fins of the radiator and if the fins disintegrate or turn to dust, stay away from the vehicle—it could signify engine problems! Also, check for corrosion around the cooling tubes. It indicates they are bad or clogged.

Rear-Wheel Drive With a rear-wheel drive, you could (when driving) put the car in second gear and go about 30 mph. Let off of the gas and if you can hear any clunking noises, the universal joints in the drive train may be worn. Listen for any kind of whining noises when you test drive an automobile. *Reminder:* Be sure to keep the radio off so you can hear any unusual noises.

Shock and Struts These absorb the roughness of the road. Take your hands and push down sharply on the trunk and hood. See if the car comes right back up and stops without bouncing. If you can get the car to bounce up and down more than once, the shocks and struts are bad and need replacing. Bad shocks/struts cause handling problems and can be dangerous.

Stars in the Windshield Check for stars in the windshield no matter how small they may appear. One bump could cause the star to crack all across the windshield.

Also, a change in temperature can make stars bigger. On a cold day, the heat from the defroster could crack it just from having a stone chip. Windshields are very expensive to replace. Do not overlook them.

Steering Try to turn the steering wheel as if you were cornering. Jiggle it back and forth and up and down. Sometimes the wheel will get loose, and if there is any kind of play at all it could indicate there is a tie rod end problem, which is very costly to repair!

Stereo System Always check the stereo system. Make sure the complete system works: the speakers, cassette, radio, CD player, etc. Buzzing speakers will drive you nuts. If the system isn't working properly and you're dealing with a car lot, make them swap the system out of another car. Then turn if off so you can complete your checklist.

Tires Look at the tires, front and back and from side to side. Check for uneven wear on either side (the tread pattern will be scuffed away). This could indicate some front-end work is needed. (At least an alignment!) Check the back tires for tire scalping. Here's how: Place your hand on the top of the tire at the ten o'clock position and run it over to the three o'clock position. Feel for smoothness in the back. If it's choppy, this indicates bad struts. Be careful of exposed metal fibers or bubbles in a badly worn tire. (They hurt when they stick your fingers!) This is extremely dangerous and could result in a tire blowout! Insist on replacement of bad tires.

Title Brand Always ask to see the title before signing anything. If the automobile was involved in a wreck or a

> Check for stars in the windshield no matter how small they may appear.

flood or was stolen, the title might be branded "R" (reconstruction).

Transmission Request to test-drive the automobile in several types of scenarios (up hills, down hills, highways, back roads, etc.). You want to feel the shifts in between all gears. Does it shift smoothly or jerkily? Does it feel shaky? If the transmission is an automatic with overdrive, be sure to take it through all of the gears, including reverse. Check the transmission fluid before you drive it. Smell the dipstick and observe the color of the fluid. If it is dark in color and you can smell a burnt odor, there may be a transmission problem. If the transmission is a manual, again take the car through every single gear including reverse. Always let go of the gear stick in between each gear. If the synchronizer isn't working, it could jump out of gear. That happens a lot when the driver has kept his/her hand on the shifter. This habit wears out the synchronizer and the shifter won't stay in gear.

Universal Joints In rear-wheel drive vehicles, listen carefully for squeaky noises when test-driving. Squeaks would indicate worn universal joints.

Valve Seals Make sure that the vehicle you are looking at has not been prestarted—you should start it up cold. Check for blue smoke or see if it smells like oil. (White smoke on a cold start is normal.) Check the exhaust pipe for black, sooty wetness. This would indicate bad valve seals. The vehicle will have oil consumption if the valve seals are leaky. Valve seal repair is an internal engine job and very costly.

Vacuum Lines Look under the hood for dry, cracked vacuum lines. This could indicate that the car has been running hot (overheating).

Water Leaks Look in the trunk and feel underneath the spare tire for wetness. This is a good indication of a wrecked unit. See if the drain plug has been removed. You don't want a wet trunk because it will rust out quickly. Also, if at all possible, run the car through a car wash to check for leaks around all of the windows, sunroof, convertible tops, etc.

Wrecked Unit If possible, have someone follow you down the road and watch the car. Observe how it drives down the road. Look for the crabwalk. That's where the front wheels are over to the right and the back wheels are over to the left (or vice versa). Basically, the back wheels aren't following the front wheels correctly. Check the doors and the door hinges. Grab the door and move it up and down to check the strength and the alignment along with the rest of the body of the automobile. Referring to the paint, check for cracks, bubbles, rough places, dull spots, over-spray, etc. Check the color of paint in the door hinges, under the hood, and in the trunk for a match. (Watch for the branded title "R".) Beware of the unbelievable spectacular deal! Always ask if the automobile has ever been involved in a wreck of any kind, whether you suspect it or not. Sometimes they will deliberately lie to you, as in the following story.

A very close friend once bought a used Nissan 300ZX. It was a beautiful midnight blue in color and he absolutely loved it. When Richard bought the car, he specifically

I know that some of you ladies are mechanical geniuses or your mechanical skills no doubt reach far beyond this chapter. Others of you aren't mechanics, but you have a vast learned knowledge about the mechanics of automobiles. If you fall into any of these categories, you should give yourself a pat on the back and be proud because many of us are totally clueless. You go girl!

asked both the sales representative and the sales manager if it had ever been wrecked. The response was an ever so anxious no.

About one year later the paint began to flake off, and lo and behold the car was *red,* not *blue.* He called the dealership and at first they said they couldn't do anything about it. He had bought the car used and signed the *as-is* document.

Richard made several phone calls to them trying to get his money back, another automobile, or some sort of rectification. His argument with them was that he specifically asked if the car had ever been wrecked and the sales team had been emphatic that it had not.

When he couldn't get any satisfaction, he talked to a couple of attorneys. Once attorneys came into the picture, the dealership was more willing to reach an equitable solution. The ultimate solution was to give Richard full credit of the 300ZX purchase price toward another vehicle of his choosing.

Because of the nature of the beast, they will say what you want to hear. The goal of the sales team is to get you into their car, and if it means lying, then so be it. *They will lie!*

There are just a few last things to remember when considering a used automobile of any type: If buying from an individual, always ask why they are selling it. Ask specific questions to determine whether it's a problem car, or whether the seller just wants to buy a new car. Has it ever been wrecked, in a flood, or stolen? If you're buying from a car lot, ask why the previous owner traded it in, and, again, ask if it was a problem car or did they just want a new car. Was it ever wrecked? Ask those questions! It's the only way you'll find out the information needed to make a good, sensible decision.

Finally, at the end of your inspection, write down everything that troubles you or needs to be repaired/replaced. If you're purchasing the vehicle from a dealer, make them sign a condition of sale listing everything you want repaired or replaced. If they won't, then use your list as a bargaining tool to get the price down, but know ahead what you're getting into. If you're purchasing from an individual, most likely it will be an as-is sale.

This chapter is not intended to instantly certify you as a mechanic, so don't pretend to be one. You'll only embarrass yourself. This chapter is intended to give you some basic and easy-to-understand information for judging the condition of an automobile.

Mechanic or not, don't settle for the typical test drive. Beware of any used car, no matter where it's coming from, including friends and relatives. I'm sure you've heard the old saying, never do business with friends or relatives . . .

There is a reason. My mother was a late bloomer when it came to driving and was in her thirties before she ever learned how. Her wanting to drive was brought on by the simple fact that she was completely dependent on my father for transportation. If she ever wanted to go anywhere, she had to get him to take her. To claim her long-desired independence, Mom decided to get her driver's license. Before she did, though, she wanted to have her own car to take the test in. She turned to Bill, her supervisor at the factory where she worked. Bill and his partner owned a small used car lot in town. Disregarding the company's policy against self-promotion, they generated many sales from the factory employees, and, naturally, Mom trusted him. One day after work she caught a ride with Bill over to his car lot to pick out her new car. Or at least it was new to her. Bill assured her that the particular car she wanted was in mint condition and didn't need a thing done to it. Not being able to drive

> Finally, at the end of your inspection, write down everything that troubles you or needs to be repaired/replaced.

Buy with your eyes wide open and listen carefully as the automobile cries out with each ailment. Smell its fumes and odors and feel its scars inside and out. Only then can you or should you draw a conclusion about its mechanical condition.

yet and being the trusting soul that she was, Mom went ahead and signed all of the papers without test-driving the car first. Because my dad worked late hours, she made arrangements with her good friend Jenny to pick it up the following day. Mom was so proud of herself. She had bought her first car, a Chevy Chevette.

As scheduled, Jenny went to pick up the car. On the way to our house, she noticed that the ride wasn't smooth. She also noticed some strange noises and a strong odor coming from underneath the hood. Immediately, she drove to a phone booth and called Mom at work. Jenny asked her if she had test-driven the car before she bought it. Mom's answer was no. She told her that she was afraid to since she didn't have her license yet. Besides, Bill assured her that the car was tip-top. Jenny warned Mom of the potential problems and suggested that the car be taken to her mechanic where it could be checked out thoroughly. Mom agreed and Jenny drove the car straight to the mechanic's shop.

The car was inspected and the mechanic made a list of things wrong to the tune of almost $2,000. The transmission was bad, the brakes were bad, the tires were worn, the alignment was all out of whack, the oil was dark and sludgy, which means it hadn't been serviced in forever, the air conditioner wasn't working properly, and there were a few other things wrong with it. Mom got a copy of the list from the mechanic and took it straight to Bill. She told him that she had totally trusted him and because he was her supervisor, she had bought the car in complete faith. She also warned him that he either take his car back immediately and fix everything on the list to her satisfaction or else she would fix him! She would not only let everyone at work know what a piece of junk he sold her, but she would turn him in to the main office, which could result in loss of his job since he was ignoring the company policy. She would also call the Better Business Bureau and report the incident. If this wasn't enough to rectify the problem, she'd notify the newspaper and the radio stations. In a small town, a business owner doesn't need any bad publicity. It can destroy them.

Bill took the car back and made all needed repairs and then personally delivered the car to our house, hoping to save face. Mom finally got her car (although not as excited about it as she originally was), and gained her independence. She finally got her license. The scorpion stung and the frog almost drowned!

CHAPTER 5

The Deal You Can Afford

When the automotive industry came up with an innovative concept like the first-time buyer program, it totally outdid itself. This particular program created great opportunities for their newly found customers (mostly young, inexperienced, extremely gullible, and, many times, desperate people) to drive away in a brand new car. More truthfully, though, this new concept laid out a beneficial design of attack for the scorpions. Often, these customers would come in with their peers, all of whom were just as anxious to drive away in a new car. One sale would evolve into two or three sales. (Peer pressure: "If he/she got one, I want one, too!")

At first, the dealer guidelines had many loopholes and were not very strict at all. The profits made were unbelievable, and due to the typical buyer's state of mind, it was an easy score for the dealer!

For example: "Hey Alison, think I'd stand half a chance of getting that car?" "Oh Sarah, I'd be so grateful to buy anything if that salesperson would just help me," "Oh my gosh, Jessica, look at that one—I'd just die for it!" And then there's Melissa—a totally hopeless case. "I don't care what it is, just get me in something."

Ya gotta be bold, ya gotta be strong, ya gotta be wiser!

Stop one minute and think about these scenarios. Joel, the salesman of the year is going to rip your pocket wide open if he hears talk like that, so don't even go there.

The first-time buyer program has been overhauled and fine-tuned along with other programs that have been developed. The restrictions and guidelines on all of them for both dealers and customers have become much more stringent! The results are less profit potential for the greed demons and more protection for consumers—an obvious plus for you.

Unfortunately for many of the early birds that were financed under the first-time buyer program, the financial weight was more than their wings could carry and they crashed. Repossession was the outcome. You gotta get the attitude right. Keep a level head on your shoulders and you'll get the deal you can afford.

Your Attitude Versus the Dealer's

Whether you're a first-time buyer, a last-time buyer, or a somewhere-in-the-middle buyer, don't let yourself get caught up in the buying process and be claimed someone's prey for the day. Pause for a moment, and compose yourself. Take precautions no matter how enticing!

You Must Be Willing to Walk Away from a Bad Deal

You must be willing to walk away from a bad deal if indeed it is a bad deal. Don't let your desires and emotions dip into your pocketbook. After all, that's what we're talking about, isn't it? Not dipping into your pocketbook and saving money. Am I sounding like a broken record yet? I hope so!

The dealer must want to put you in the vehicle.

The Dealer Must Want to Put You in the Vehicle

On the flip side of the coin, be calm. Don't be too stand-offish or unsociable. Make friends with salespeople. Remember the attitudes. You want them to work for you, not against you. The more pleasant, comfortable, and confident you are, the easier your goal will be to attain. Don't be The Know-It-All, Ms. Be-Careful-My-Boyfriend-Is-Here, or Ms. This-Is-My-Father. Such behavior will only get you blown out of the water (a tactic used on customers who possess dominating, harsh, and unrealistic attitudes and expectations). The dealership will quote such outrageously high prices and swear that's the best they can do with the sole intent of making the customer leave. Dealers perceive customers with attitudes as nothing but troublemakers and would rather not deal with them.

Negotiating Points

There's that word that so many of us seem to be afraid of. Why? Perhaps it is our fear of the unknown or the lack of know-how. What does negotiate mean? Negotiating is simply coming to terms or coming to an agreement (challenging a dealer on price). A successful negotiation will benefit all parties. So why is it difficult for some and easy for others?

"I'M NOT READY TO BUY . . . . ."

> Knowledge
> is power
> and power
> is strength.
> Power and
> strength
> equals an
> attitude of
> confidence!

An individual's personality does have some degree of effect on his or her ability to negotiate. For example, if someone is very strong-minded and resistant to others, the negotiating odds are in their favor. That person will have distinct traits of forwardness and persistence and usually will be very confident. However, if someone is not so strong-minded, is easily influenced by others and less confident, the odds are less favorable and that person will have to put forth more effort and step outside of his or her comfort zone. *Knowledge is the key.*

Up-Front Deposits

Think of negotiating as a game of will power in that your strength of mind will give you the ammunition needed to win the games that car dealers play. One of the first mind games you will have to endure that actually takes place right in the beginning of the negotiating stage is the request for a cash deposit or an *up-front deposit*, ($500, $1,000, $2,000, etc.) If you don't have the cash, dealers will try to push you to leave a check, credit cards, or even your driver's license (as a last resort).

Supposedly, this shows them that you are a serious buyer and that you want to do business. Sales representatives will claim that they must have some kind of deposit in order to approach the sales manager or he won't even look at the deal, and there certainly won't be any negotiating.

Get real! What an out-and-out lie! It's simply another game of control. They feel that as long as they have your money in their pocket, you won't be going anywhere anytime soon. The problem with giving them an up-front deposit is that if you leave your money with them to hold the car so you can "go home and sleep on it," chances are, you won't get it back if you end up not buying. Their reason always is, "We held our car for you." There was another customer looking at it but because there was a hold on it, the customer went elsewhere to buy. You cost them a sale.

I once accepted a beautiful diamond watch as a deposit from the wife of a prominent local businessman. It was an expensive one at that. She wanted me to hold a brand new Pontiac Trans-Am for her because it was going to be a birthday present for her granddaughter. Her husband usually handled all of their business affairs but was out of town and had asked her to do some auto shopping while he was gone. She had left her checkbook and credit cards at home in another handbag and all she had was her watch. We told her that there were other people looking at the car and if she wanted us to hold it for her, she would have to leave something. She handed me her watch and we accepted it. It was placed in the dealership safe until her husband returned to view the car.

Because of who these people were, we did not want to let her leave without some type of deposit, even if it was her watch. Obviously, she was going to come back for that. They were serious buyers and could easily drive down the road to another dealership and buy. A few days later, they returned and bought the Trans-Am for their granddaughter and made one young lady a very happy birthday girl!

If someone asks you for a deposit before you've committed to buy or before you've even discussed price, tell them absolutely not. If they can't discuss price without first having your money in their hand (no matter what form of deposit it is), you don't need to be there. Go somewhere else. Besides, nowadays it's dangerous to place your credit cards and driver's license in someone else's possession. They can find out much more about you than

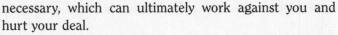

The True
Discount
versus the
Almighty
Hype

necessary, which can ultimately work against you and hurt your deal.

In order to overcome negotiating obstacles skillfully, you need to know and totally comprehend the factors contributing to this process. Some of these factors include discounts, rebates, holdbacks, addendum stickers, and trade-ins. It's time to play "Let's make a deal!"

Discounts

Discounting is selling at prices below those set by manufacturers. One has to learn to recognize a true discount versus the almighty hype (questionable claims of advertising).

Check out this conservative scenario (to simplify all illustrations, I will omit tax and license): Elizabeth, an inexperienced buyer, has test-driven a new car and decided she wants it. The MSRP, which includes the destination charge (a delivery charge from the factory to the dealer), is $16,485 plus another ludicrously inflated $600 for rustproofing, undercoating, paint sealant, and fabric protection. These extras that are presumably added to the addendum sticker generally cost the dealer less than $100.

Now the total is $17,085. If Heather offers to sell Elizabeth the car for $16,185 showing a discount of $900, is Elizabeth getting a good deal? Add the more realistic cost of $100 for the extras to the MSRP, and the total is $16,585. Deduct the selling price from the total and there you have it, a difference of $400, not $900. Great discount, huh? Remember that the average markup of an automobile is around 8–15 percent depending on price range. (Luxury lines such as Mercedes, BMW, Porsche, and Rolls Royce have a considerably higher markup). If the markup on the car Elizabeth wants to buy is 12 percent of the

MSRP, which equals $1,978.20, then the actual cost of the unit is $14,506.80. Take $16,485.00 minus the 12 percent markup of $1,978.20 and that equals $14,506.80. If Elizabeth throws the towel in without a fight, Heather has profited for the dealer $1,678.20 big ones (sale price of $16,185 minus cost of $14,506.80). It doesn't stop there. Don't forget about the rebates, dealer bonuses, holdbacks, finance profits, trade-ins, etc.

Dealers can make much more profit if you let them!

Rebates

Rebates, also referred to as cash back or refunds, are deductions from an amount to be paid or a return of part of an amount already paid. For years dealers and manufacturers have successfully utilized rebates as a means of luring customers to their products in hopes of boosting sales. Now that these costly incentives have become customary and are a way of life, automakers want to discontinue them. However, competition and demanding consumers are preventing that from happening (at least for the time being). How much longer will rebates be offered? Who knows, but for now take advantage of them while you still can.

Customer Rebates

Customer rebates are advertised by manufacturers and dealers on national and local television, radio, and in the newspaper. Rebates of $500 and $1,000 are the most commonly seen, but with higher-priced units the rebate can go up to $2,000, $3,000, or more. Special low finance rates are normally offered in conjunction with rebates, but customers have to choose one or the other. However, once in a while a manufacturer will give both rebates and low interest rates, which makes the decision-making and buying process much easier for the customer and the savings even greater. Let's assume that Kelly is the buyer now and she is more experienced in automotive shopping than Elizabeth. The manufacturer is offering $1,000 rebate or low financing. Kelly chooses to go with the rebate because she knows she can get the same low finance rates at her personal bank. She has done her homework! Heather offers to sell her the car for $15,585 using the rebate as down-stroke (down payment). Is this a good deal?

Nope! Kelly realizes that all Heather is doing is deducting the $1,000 rebate from the $16,585 (MSRP) and not discounting the price one penny. Kelly is much smarter than that and counters with an offer of $14,100 assigning the rebate (cash back) to the dealer, which makes a total of $15,100. Now that's much better. How much profit is made at this price? Take $15,100 minus the actual dealer cost of $14,506.80 equals $593.20. That's a fair profit, wouldn't you say? Well that depends. Is there a dealer rebate?

Dealer Rebates

> Dealer rebates are essentially money bonuses given to dealers from the manufacturers.

Dealer rebates are essentially money bonuses given to dealers from the manufacturers. Amounts vary as with customer rebates ($300, $500, $1,000, $2,000, and more). They are not advertised because this is gravy money and extra profit that goes directly into the dealer's pocket. It gives dealers not only more bargaining room but also more incentive to promote and sell particular models that the manufacturers wish to move. If you see or hear an advertisement offering unbelievably low prices of, for example, $100 under invoice, I guarantee there is a dealer rebate. In our scenario, if there were a $1,000 dealer rebate, then the total profit would be $1,593.20. Room to wheel and deal, don't you think?

Holdbacks

Domestic and some foreign automobiles have what's called holdback. A holdback is basically bonus or kickback money that automotive manufacturers award dealers on each new unit they sell. This does add to their pot of gold but is primarily to help pay for overhead and advertising expenses. The method by which holdback money is paid depends upon the arrangement a dealer has with the manufacturer. It could be issued monthly, quarterly, semiannually, etc. The amount of holdback is generally around 3–6 percent of MSRP and just like the markup, the lower the price, the lower the holdback and the higher the price, the higher the holdback. In our scenario, that would be $989.10 (assuming a 6 percent holdback of $16,485) for a total profit now of $2,582.30. OUCH! And we haven't even entered the finance office yet.

More dealer rebates.

Dealer Add-Ons (Addendum)

The aftermarket chemicals, products, and additional equipment that are added to an automobile either at the dealership in the service department or subcontracted out to another company are called add-ons. These additions and their costs are listed on an addendum sticker and placed alongside the factory sticker showing a new total price (MSRP plus the add-ons). There are two different types of dealer add-ons you should be familiar with.

Hard Add-Ons

These are the valid additions: pinstripes, tinted windows, sunroofs, deluxe radio systems, step-bumpers, bedliners, spoilers, graphics (art designs normally seen on pick-ups and vans), special wheels, etc.

Soft Add-Ons

These are a joke. These non-valid additions include items such as leakage and seepage or snake oil, the slang terminology for undercoating, rustproofing, paint sealant, and fabric protection.

Pay close attention to the addendum stickers. Make doubly sure that the hard add-ons listed have actually been added. If there is an extra $200 charge for a sound system upgrade from cassette to CD, make sure the upgrade has been completed. Also pay attention to what kind of sound system the factory sticker has listed. Sometimes a dealer will swap out radios from one unit to another in order to close a sale. Are pinstripes listed? Have they been done or are they complete? If there is a charge for a special tailgate, a different bumper, or a bedliner, make sure it has actually been added. Another thing to look for is an addendum sticker that has been typed up ahead of time and placed on units, but for some reason the work got overlooked or somehow strangely forgotten. If that's the case, I assure you that the majority of dealers will not bring it up unless you do.

As for soft add-ons, just remember the ludicrous prices that dealers charge for so-called protection products can be grossly inflated, and though they may be listed as having been done, again many times are not. Actually, 99.999 percent of the time, you are charged for the protection products and they have not been applied. (Just a warning!) If you are paying for the protection products, make sure they are applied in your presence.

The $600 amount that I used in the illustrations is actually a very low figure. I've worked at dealerships where the standard charge was as much as $1,500. It's just added cushion to enable dealers to show discounts without really giving discounts (the almighty hype). Over the last ten years manufacturers have vastly improved the materials their automobiles are made from. The results have been superior products, and an astonishing decrease of corrosion and paint problems. And most if not all automobiles are now precoated with the highest quality protection products straight from the factory. So why do dealers need to apply it again? They don't need to. Like I said, it's just more *profit for the pocket!*

Actually, some of the aftermarket protection products do more harm than good! For example, the fabric protection can make the seat covers more stain-prone. Some of the rustproofing and undercoating products can cause a chemical reaction with the factory applied protection, thus causing a breakdown in the materials the automobile is made of. And paint sealant can really mess up a paint job. Be careful!

Your Trade-in Vehicle

You absolutely must know what your trade-in is worth (wholesale) before challenging any dealer. A dealer's idea of a trade-in allowance is $0.00. They will try to get away with this if they think they can. Believe me, they will try. "Thou shalt pay full retail (or more) for my goods and I shall only give ye wholesale (or less) for thy goods," saith the dealer.

One of the first things any sales team will attempt to do is to psychologically devalue your jalopy. Your trade-in may not be a jalopy at all, but by the time they're finished doing their number, you won't be so sure what you have. Psychological devaluation is achieved by using one of the oldest tricks of the trade, the clipboard/hands-on routine. As you watch, attentively observing every little movement, the appraiser and/or sales manager (the people that supposedly know—the ones with authority—hmmm) from the

> You absolutely must know what your trade-in is worth (wholesale) before challenging any dealer.

used car department will walk around your car with a clipboard, critically evaluating it. They will write things down and point out all that is or isn't wrong with your car inside and out. They will scratch bad spots in the paint along with a whole list of other things. They'll rub the tires to make you think they're worn out, turn the engine on and off repeatedly because of "unusual noises" heard, check underneath the car and hood for leaks, corrosion, spray paint (yes, spray paint) and whatever else they might think of. (If your trade-in has ever been repainted, one might see some overspray.)

All of these dramatics are to make customers extremely nervous, confused, and definitely unsure of the condition and value of their car. And does it ever work! Even if customers know the value of their trade-in without a shadow of a doubt, this Broadway production that the "actors" deliver will still make one doubtful and unsure, which leads me back to my first statement. You gotta know what ya got! When you do, you can take the lead and improvise your own skit lines into their production.

Shop Your Trade-in First

As you already know, you can call your local license bureau, your bank, go to the library or bookstore, or jump on-line on the Internet and cruise through the automotive Web pages to get an estimated value for your trade-in. The sources that these locations mostly use are the *Kelley Blue Book* or its equivalent and the *Official N.A.D.A. Used Car Guide* (National Automobile Dealers Association), which lists the base, retail, and loan values. Options such as air conditioning, cassette or CD, power windows, power locks, tilt wheel, and cruise control are itemized individually with their values to the side of them. They are added to the retail and loan value.

There is also an addition or deduction for low and high mileage. Average mileage does not affect the value. When dealers sell a used automobile (with or without a trade-in) and they need to figure taxes or need to know a particular loan value, they reach for the *Official N.A.D.A. Used Car Guide*, but when it comes to trade-in allowances, that's altogether different! They refer to the *Black Book Guide*, which lists wholesale values and categorizes automobiles based on their condition: rough, average, clean, and extra clean. The *Black Book Guide* also itemizes the options, and there is the addition or deduction for low or high mileage. And the same rule applies: Average mileage does not affect the value.

Your trade-in is very much like an individual in the sense that it has its own distinctive traits and flaws. So in order to acquire a true monetary worth, you are much better off shopping your trade-in. Do the used car lot thing and gather wholesale appraisals. (You're going to sell it, remember?) The appraisals will probably vary some but should be relatively close and most definitely more on target. Now it's time to go to the auction block. Who is going to give you the best bid? Would you be better off to sell your vehicle outright to an individual, trade it to a dealer on your next purchase, unload it to a wholesaler or used car lot that specializes in older models, or perhaps sell it to a junkyard junkie for parts? Who's gonna win? You can call one of those consumer hot line services to get a value on your trade-in, but there will be a fee, and how can you get an accurate figure when they haven't seen it? That will always be a dealer's reasoning and like it or not, they are right!

Wholesale Value

Market value, *Black Book* value, and actual cash value are all the same as wholesale value. If you unload

"Uh, I hate to say this but I think your automobile is about to fall apart. Just look at the list of things we found wrong with it." PSYCHE! They Wish!

your vehicle to a wholesaler or used car lot, you are not going to be in a bargaining position and you'll get the low, low dollar (wholesale or less.) Take it or leave it. You're asking them and they won't lose any sleep over not having your pride and joy in their possession.

The junkyard junkie operates what is properly known as a salvage yard. Salvage yards are major profit industries. They buy wrecks and old clunkers to recycle and sell parts off of that are still good or salvageable: engines, transmissions, mufflers, starters, doors, seats, panels, mirrors, and anything they can make a dollar on. Their customers are service departments, service stations, independently and commercially owned automotive repair centers, and individuals. Make no mistake, you will not get much money from a salvage yard, but if you have one of those aged putt-putts that has to be towed every time you drive it and dealers are showing no enthusiasm whatsoever about taking it in on trade, at least you have an alternative.

Retail Value

If you decide to trade your automobile in, it's possible to get more than wholesale but you have to stick with the plan of negotiating a straight-out purchase price first before bringing your cards (your trade-in) to the table. By doing so, the deal is much easier to follow and you can see more clearly if you're being had or if they are actually giving you retail value. For a used vehicle purchase, beware of any immediate $3,000 to $4,000 discounts or trade-in allowance guarantees regardless of what kind of trade you have or the condition it's in. The dealer might as well hang up a flashing neon sign that says "Drastically Marked Up Merchandise, Come and Get It". Even after discounts and trade-in allowances have been deducted from the selling price, there will still be much more room to

For a used vehicle purchase, beware of any immediate $3,000 to $4,000 discounts or trade-in allowance guarantees regardless of what kind of trade you have or the condition it's in.

come down. For new vehicle purchases, keep in mind that the discounts, dealer rebates/bonuses, and holdbacks all have a part in negotiating. When your purchase is written up, if the discount is not deducted right from the top, it will probably be added to your trade-in allowance. By knowing what your trade is worth, you will be able to tell how much they are actually allowing you for your trade and how much the price is being discounted.

Let's say Hunter is buying a new pickup truck with an MSRP of $18,500. The markup margin is 12 percent ($2,220) making the dealer invoice $16,280. His trade-in is actually worth $3,000 wholesale. If Heather offers to sell him the truck for a trading difference of $15,500 (showing him a $3,000 trade-in allowance) did she discount any? Obviously not! Now, let's say the deal is written up showing Hunter a $4,000 trade-in allowance, leaving a balance of $14,500. That's only a $1,000 discount added to his trade-in allowance and he knows the dealer can do better than that. If Hunter can squeeze an additional $1,500 out of Heather for his trade-in, making it a total trade-in allowance of $5,500 for a final trading difference of $13,000, then he is definitely getting a favorable deal. The trade-in allowance breakdown would be as follows: $3,000 actual cash value + $2,220 discount (the 12 percent markup) + $330 out of the dealers pocket. Will the dealer make anything? $13,000 difference + $3,000 actual cash value for the trade-in, + $925 for holdback (5 percent of MSRP) = $16,925−$16,280 (dealer invoice) = $645 (dealer profit not including any dealer rebate or bonuses.) That is still a great buy for a new pickup truck.

If there is a $1,000 customer rebate, then the $1,000 should be deducted from $13,000 and Hunter would only pay a difference of $12,000. And just so you'll know, when a dealer gives more than wholesale value for a trade-in, it's

Note: Get your keys back immediately following the appraisal of your trade-in, and refuse to discuss any price whatsoever until they are back in your possession! Don't be surprised when the dealer hesitates to give them back. This is one of their ways of controlling you. As long as your keys are in the dealer's possession, you can't go anywhere.

Oh-h-h . . .
I'm so
confused!

called trade-in overallowance. That's one way of getting retail value. Are you totally confused? Don't feel bad if you are because it's very easy to get lost in all of these figures. That's why you have to negotiate a straight-out purchase price first, and then bring in the trade. Call it a preventive measure!

Special Note: Here's an inside scoop on trucks.

In the past, dealers were not required to put the manufacturer's price sticker on the window, thus giving them the perfect opportunity to make up their own prices and increase them by thousands. Supposedly this practice has been stopped. But just to be on the safe side—if you're in the market for a new truck, find the one you want first. Write down all of the specs (model, equipment, packages, etc.), then leave and go do some major homework.

Sell It Yourself

Another way of getting retail value for your vehicle, as long as it is in good condition, is to sell it to an individual. You do not want to knowingly unload a pile of junk on someone, especially a friend. That would not be right nor would it be safe for your health if you catch my drift. Many potential buyers look for dependable used transportation in classified ads or some type of used car magazine. By selling it yourself, you might get retail value, but there is a downside.

First of all, there's the cost for advertising (and you should advertise in several publications if you want to be effective). You must be reachable at all times for your best chance of selling this way, which means giving out your day and night phone numbers. You must make yourself available to show the car and deal with the hassles of always keeping it looking good and riding along on test drives (you're always taking a risk when you let a total stranger drive your automobile). I advise you to only accept cash, a certified check, or a money order. Absolutely do not take a personal check!

When you do sell your vehicle, make sure the buyer transfers it immediately out of your name into theirs properly and pays all taxes due. You don't want to get stuck with a big tax bill a year later. And last, do not get involved with financing it for the buyer!

Ever heard of T-R-O-U-B-L-E?

One-Price Shopping/ The No-Dicker Sticker

Before I enlighten you on one-price shopping, a little history lesson is in order. Over the past several decades, thousands of automotive dealers and their sales teams, the bad apples in the business, managed to infiltrate the industry with their heartless, greed-stricken, and dishonest methods for achieving sky-high profits. *Highway Robbery!*

As these so-called sales professionals began moving from dealer to dealer training new recruits, their devious rules, lack of ethics, and underhanded tactics became the norm and spread through the industry like a plague. Unfortunately for the manufacturers, this reflected upon them as well. It wasn't until later that dealers began realizing the consequences of their actions when customers would return to trade again and couldn't because they were so far upside down (owing much more on their trade-in than it was worth).

What did dealers expect when they were not only hitting the jackpot on the actual sale of the automobile,

Wonder,
wonder,
wonder,
wonder,
who, who
wrote the
book of
"RIP OFF"?

but charging customers outlandish interest rates for sixty, seventy-two, and eighty-four months? Dealers were pocketing as much as $1,000, $1,500, or more over actual cost for extended warranties. Also, credit life and accidental health insurance premiums were added to loans, which cost two to three times more than what customers could have gotten through their own insurance agent. These potential repeat buyers were roadkill and were very disturbed when they realized that their good buddy Joe stuck it to them. They couldn't trade again unless a very large down payment was made (which many didn't have). As these unethical methods have continued through the present day, dealers continue to be faced with rebellious and resentful consumers everywhere.

Thanks to the bad apple movement, auto industry reputations suffered immensely from their own self-inflicted wounds. The automotive retail world had to build a road to salvation and come up with a quick fix, a bandage to bind old wounds, bury the past, and start anew. The quick fix had to sound angelic to the consumers and put them at ease. It had to save a potential customer from that dreadful negotiation process, and voilà, the one-price shopping or the no-dicker sticker approach was born.

Though the one-price shopping/no-dicker sticker approach is totally hassle free, you are choosing to pay a higher price! This excludes Saturn products (new units) where each model line has one non-negotiable selling price. It also excludes the factory-regulated, non-negotiable, one-price specials that other manufacturers occasionally offer on specific models that aren't moving in hopes of boosting sales. Factory regulated is the key.

If the deal is factory regulated, the price is consistent among all dealers. However, more and more dealers (new and used) are adopting the one-price method, but there is a *big* difference. That so-called one price is set by the individual dealer, not the factory, and is not consistent with other dealers. This means that there is the potential to go down the road and find the same automobile for less money.

One-Price Shopping/The No-Dicker Sticker—It ain't all that!

To make it easier, just remember that if you are buying one of those one-price-no-hassle specials, profits are locked in. Every unit is a score and the dealer always wins. With the negotiating approach, you have the opportunity to challenge the dealer to a game. You can control your own destination. Sometimes the dealer will win and sometimes the dealer will lose because customers can always offer less money, and there's always going to be another dealer waiting for you who wants your money just as bad—if not more! So you see, one-price shopping is not always the best bargain!

You can kiss the great discount good bye, and as for those of you who are buying a new automobile and depend on rebates for down payment, forget it! You can also kiss them goodbye. The price on the window might include a discount, but you can definitely get a much better price negotiating for yourself if you are willing to roll the dice. Furthermore, don't expect to get a penny over wholesale value for your trade-in. It ain't gonna happen! So what does one do?

You either challenge the dealer to his game and negotiate your best buy, or you take the "high" way, what the dealer offers on the one-price/no-dicker sticker, hassle-free approach, knowing full well that it's probably not the best buy. Is it worth it? Only you can decide.

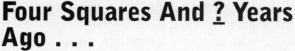

> Dig a lot
> deeper in
> the well,
> boys!

Four Squares And <u>?</u> Years Ago . . .

The retail auto world came up with the *four square* method, used to throw customers into a state of complete perplexity (total confusion) during the negotiating process. If a sales representative pulls out a sheet of paper and begins to divide it into four squares, get up and walk out immediately!

They will ask you four questions (one for each square):

1. What price do you want to pay?
2. What is your desired payment?
3. How much do you want for your trade-in, if you have one?
4. How much of a down payment do you have?

Your sales representative will write each response down in each of the squares and then disappear for a while. When he or she returns, you'll find that your $15,000 desired purchase price has been crossed out. It's gonna take $25,000 to own this jewel. And forget the $250 a month payment because it's $500 a month. Your trade-in you thought was worth all the money in the world, is only worth (-)$1,000 in their eyes, and if you think a $200 down payment will get you behind the wheel, don't count on it. Come on, fork it over—$5,000 big ones!

Have you died yet? Has your heart stopped beating? That's the plan. They want to shock the <u>X#!O</u> out of you in an effort to completely throw you off track. The figures are bogus! They don't mean anything. They just grabbed them out of thin air.

	YOU SAY	THEY SAY
Price	$15,000	$25,000
Payment	$250/month	$500/month
Trade	All the money	
	in the world	(-)$1,000
Down-		
Payment	$200	$5,000

Four Square
Method—
What a joke!

In an effort to get some sort of commitment before writing up any type of structured deal, they will address each individual square separately, badgering you repeatedly and attempting to raise your price to their price and your payment to their payment. They will give you as little trade-in allowance as possible and squeeze as much down payment out of you as they can, and all the while you're totally in the dark, confused, and destined to pay *thousands* more than necessary. Don't play this game or your well will surely run dry!

Behind Closed Doors (Roll 'Em—Action!)

What? You ask. It's all about more role-playing. You have been at the dealership for several hours and now you're getting down to the nitty-gritty of negotiating. You and the sales representative have already been haggling over price for quite some time and you're still $2,000 apart. ROLL 'EM—ACTION, time to role-play again. Looking ever so deeply and sincerely into your eyes, you hear those sugar-coated magical words in a smooth comforting voice straight out of the horses mouth: "Well, I want you to know that I'm really on your side and I am going to do everything in my power to get our price closer to your price. I know just how badly you want that car. Let me go to my manager and see what I can do. I'm not promising anything, but I'll do my best."

Yeah right! He gets up out of his chair, marches directly into his sales manager's office as if he rules the world, and then closes the door. The clock ticks on and on and on. You're beginning to get uptight and feel very queasy. You're thinking that the representative must be working hard for you because he has been gone for so long.

If you were a fly on the wall for one day, you would be dumbfounded if you heard the terrible things that were said about customers behind those ever so high and mighty closed doors. This is supposed to be the time when your sales representative is working for you. He's on your side, right? Wrong! Actually, besides all of the offensive comments thrown around, they discuss anything and everything but what should be discussed (your deal). The additional conversation is not only for visual effect, but it racks up those minutes on the clock so that it appears as if they are making a tremendous effort on your behalf to get that price down. It's more like twenty long minutes of small talk and five short seconds of price-cutting. Don't be fooled. Here are some examples of the typical show-time script said behind closed doors, all of which are drawn from my memory bank:

⚿ Hey buddy, are you going to the game this weekend? It's a double-header and I have two extra tickets. You wanna go? (Gouge these suckers and we'll take the money and bet on the game.) It'll be great!

Comments behind closed doors.

- Man, did you see the hooters on that woman? She'd knock your eyeballs out of their sockets with those things if you got too close.

- Stick it to them and don't come off the price any at all. That <u>X#!O***</u> is giving me a hard time.

- The guys are going out tonight for a few drinks after work to see what we can get into. You wanna take a load off and join us? It'll get your mind off of all these idiots that have been in here today.

- Did I show you the pictures of the new boat I'm buying at the end of the month? Do me a favor and keep that price up there, would ya? I need the extra commission for my down payment.

- Man she's gorgeous! Give her a good deal.

- Oh, that customer is so ugly, they don't deserve to get a good deal.

- My customer is brain dead, totally clueless. Let's crucify her. She won't know the difference.

- Well, what else can we talk about? I've been in here fifteen minutes. Think I've stayed long enough? I don't want them to get suspicious or anything.

I think you get the picture, especially if you have any kind of imagination at all. It only gets worse. These remarks are very kind compared to some of the things that are said. The mentality of the remarks along with wasting your precious time is not only pitiful and merciless, but ridiculous as well. All of this role-playing gives the appearance that they are working for you. It's just part of the games that car dealers play.

CHAPTER 6

Payment Options

Cash

Just as it's important to understand your needs and desires, it's equally important to know which method of payment best fits your pocket. One obvious
method is with cash. If you are fortunate enough to be a cash buyer, you first
need to consider both the pros and the cons. Is paying cash for your purchase
going to benefit you more than financing your purchase? If your funds are
invested in CDs, money-market funds, savings, profit sharing, stocks, bonds,
or some other form of capital gain and you are getting a good return, do you
really want to spend your hard-earned dollars, your inheritance, or whatever
the case may be? Or could you come out ahead by financing?

Is the interest you would earn on your investment over a three- to four-
year period going to be more or less than the interest you would pay out on
a three- to four-year loan? If the earnings would be more, you should consider keeping your investment intact and taking out a low-interest loan. If
your earnings would be less, then perhaps you should follow through with
your plan to pay cash.

Your situation may be that money is no object and you were fortunate
enough to be born into a world of riches and jewels, or perhaps you won the
lottery. In that case, why worry? Pay cash and enjoy! You might be a very
successful business professional who has worked extremely hard to get

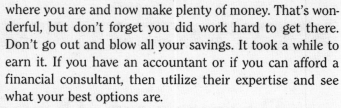

Invest as well as spend wisely!

where you are and now make plenty of money. That's wonderful, but don't forget you did work hard to get there. Don't go out and blow all your savings. It took a while to earn it. If you have an accountant or if you can afford a financial consultant, then utilize their expertise and see what your best options are.

On the other hand, you might be someone who is retired or who is widowed and on a fixed income (retirement pension, social security, disability). You have managed to save some money throughout the years and it's earning interest for you, but due to the cost of living you have to manage your money very carefully. Payments simply do not fit into your tight budget. If you financed your purchase but had to withdraw the payment every month from your savings account it would defeat the purpose of investing. In this case, if you have the money, pay up. Cash is your best option!

Own Source (Personal Bank/ Credit Union)

If you decide to finance your purchase, be sure to do your homework first. Call your personal bank and other local banks in your hometown. Inquire about their current interest rates, financing terms, and qualifying requirements. If you're a member of a credit union, call them as well. Credit unions can be most helpful. They always offer competitive interest rates to their members, and sometimes will even offer that blue-light special. ("Attention all credit union shoppers, today we are offering free credit life insurance for choosing to finance with us. And for your convenience, we have pre-arranged a credit union sale especially for you this weekend only with the local dealers. On selected models, pricing will run as low as $100 over invoice.")

If your bank or credit union has the cheapest rates, then let them (not the dealer) process the loan directly! If the dealer just so happens to do business with your bank or credit union, they will try to convince you to let them draw up the finance papers. Don't do it! Indirect financing with the dealership is just another way for them to make money. They get a kickback. I assure you that if you go through the dealer, you will pay a higher interest rate and have a higher payment, even though it is on your bank or credit union's contract.

Dealer Finance/Lease

Sales representatives, sales managers, and finance managers will all try to persuade every customer to finance or lease with them because of the extra profit potential. Keeping this in mind, check out the dealer finance/lease menu and be open to suggestions. Many times they will actually have better interest rates than you are able to get. Just like pricing though, you have to negotiate the rate down. Whatever the case may be, do not lose control and do not let them smooth talk you into doing something really stupid that's gonna cost you a lot more money in the long run, such as longer-term financing or leasing when you are absolutely not a lease candidate.

Realize that the longer you finance, the more you owe on your loan due to the additional interest, and thus you pay much more for your automobile than it's actually worth. Keep the finance term as short as possible and yet affordable. Leasing? Do you have this lifetime ritual of

> Sales representatives, sales managers, and finance managers will all try to persuade every customer to finance or lease with them because of the extra profit potential.

renting a different automobile every two to three years faithfully forever and ever, throwing your money over the side of a ship into the ocean? If not, and you like the concept of ownership, or you drive your car into the ground and rack up a trillion gazillion miles, stay away from leasing! It will cost you dearly!

Secondary Banks and Finance Companies

There might be circumstances in which you truly need the dealership's assistance in financing an automobile, the one you so desperately need or want. Let's say that you turned to your own sources for a loan but came up totally empty-handed due to having very limited credit and not having anyone to cosign with you. Possibly you had previous credit problems and you are currently trying to work your way through a bad spot. In these situations a dealer will usually be more apt to get you financed either through a secondary bank or a finance company that finances high-risk customers. You still have to meet certain criteria and requirements to qualify, such as verifiable income, job, residency, and down payment.

First-Time/ Graduate Buyer

Anyone that has never financed an automobile before, or anyone that has either recently graduated from college or who will be graduating within the academic semester is in luck. (A diploma or written verification is required.) There absolutely cannot be any derogatory (bad) credit on your

> There might be circumstances in which you truly need the dealership's assistance in financing an automobile.

credit file such as late credit card payments or late loan payments of any kind. Almost every automotive finance company has special programs for the first-time buyer and college graduate. The same rules apply. A customer must meet the specific criteria and requirements to qualify. Length of residency, ability to pay the loan back, and down payment are all very important determining factors.

CHAPTER 7

Financing Within Your Budget

L et's face it, a dollar will only stretch so far, yet sadly enough every year millions of people from all walks of life bite off more than they can chew. They spend more than they have, overextending far beyond their ability to pay back, and wake up one morning buried beneath so much financial commitment that they're doomed for financial despair. The results: persistent harassing phone calls from creditors and collection agencies, repossessions of homes, automobiles, and other personal belongings. Bankruptcies, judgments, and liens are also part of this harsh and ugly picture, all of which lead to the destruction of one's credit and integrity and the loss of financial privileges for what could seem like a lifetime. And if that's not enough, financial despair also bleeds into the personal realm, turning one's world upside down. Relationships that are dearest to the heart are often severed, ending in broken homes, irreparable friendships, and loss of jobs. In some cases, there is the horrifying, tragic reality of death caused by suicide or acts of raging violence ending in homicide.

I know that this sounds heavy-duty, but finding yourself buried in debt can have a permanent impact on your life. For those of you who have walked the paths of heavy debt and managed to survive, you've carried the cross of pain and suffering. You've worn the coat of humility and embarrassment, and

> Thou shalt walk through the valley of the shadow of "Financial Despair" if self-discipline and good old-fashioned common sense are not applied when it comes to money.

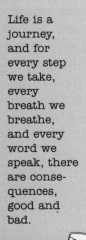

> Life is a journey, and for every step we take, every breath we breathe, and every word we speak, there are consequences, good and bad.

experienced the loss of dignity and pride. You've weathered the storms of starting over and you know that it is possible to overcome if you try hard enough.

Use sound judgement. Manage your money wisely and stay within your budget! Don't take for granted your financial privileges, and whatever you do, don't spend money that's simply not there. You don't want to walk through the valley of the shadow of financial despair. Now that I've alerted you to the importance of financing within your budget, there are definitely things you can do to secure better financial arrangements that will obviously help you to stay within your means.

The Interest Rate Game with Winners and (So-Called) Losers

Dealers have become manipulating masters of the interest rate game through the years. They will do their best to find out what kind of interest rate you are able to obtain before quoting you their interest rate. Why? They want to charge as high a rate as possible without losing your loan to another finance source, such as your own personal bank or credit union, so they can stuff their pockets with more money! For example, a dealer's lowest rate, called the buy rate (the rate at which a dealer is charged to borrow money from a lender), might be 8 percent for a forty-eight-month loan. If you tell them you can get 11 percent through your source for the same term, they might in turn charge you 10.75 percent. At 10.75 percent, the dealer is still competitive and less than your source, yet will earn 2.75 percent profit over the duration of the loan. Profit a dealer makes from the interest is called *dealer reserve*.

Basically, this rate game is the same kind of ridiculous, nerve-wracking ritual that the sales team puts you through when negotiating for a price, and if you don't stay focused and listen carefully, you'll end up paying a higher rate than necessary!

One factor that definitely plays a big part in what kind of rate you'll be offered is your credit standing. If you're one of those winners with good credit, you'll be classified as a low-risk customer and placed in a low-risk category. No doubt you will be offered lower rates, but don't think for one second that you won't be a game piece just because you have good credit.

If you're one of the so-called losers with borderline credit (limited to marginal) or bad credit, you'll be classified as a high-risk customer, placed in a high-risk category, and, yes, charged higher interest rates. Unfortunately, these are the customers that are most often at the mercy of the dealer. They have almost no say when it comes to rate unless they're able to obtain financing elsewhere. So whatever category you happen to fall into, "winners or losers," explore your options first. Find out if the options are plentiful or limited, or if indeed you truly are at the mercy of the dealer. Know that the lower your interest rate is, the lower your payment will be and the higher your interest rate is, the higher your payment will be. Now, just like the price, negotiate the rate down.

Note: Remember, unless a dealer is quoting a special low interest rate that is being offered by the manufacturer (2.9, 4.9, 6.9, etc.), the rate is negotiable. And of course you can always threaten to *shop elsewhere* if they won't lower it.

> "Everybody is a game piece and everybody plays," saith the dealer.

> We're all winners. Sometimes we just get lost and drive down the wrong road.

The Credit Application (Qualifying)

Have you ever heard the saying that the truth shall find you out? When filling out credit applications, false information knowingly reported can be cause for immediate turn-down! If you already have an existing loan and it's discovered that you misrepresented some information (lied on the credit application), it could mean a demand for an immediate payback plus a big penalty!

Believe me, everything is verified. Providing as much complete, truthful, and detailed information as possible in the beginning will certainly help to expedite the application processing time.

Have the following written down and readily available for the finance manager or loan officer prior to entering their office:

1. *Length of Residency*—For renters/lessees list the name and phone number of your landlord or realtor. For homeowners, list the name and phone number of your mortgage company or the individual you're purchasing from directly.

2. *Employer/Length of Employment*—List the company you work for, immediate boss/supervisor, job title, and earnings (gross and net). List any additional income you might receive or earn and the source from where it comes, such as additional jobs, investment profits, child support, etc. Customers most likely will be asked to provide proof of all income (two most recent pay stubs or latest tax returns), so bring proof.

3. *Asset Accounts*—List all checking and savings account numbers, money markets, trust funds, bonds, IRAs, etc., along with account balances.

4. *Debts*—Be sure to list all of your monthly obligations (like rent, mortgage, personal loans,
auto/motorcycle/boat loans, credit cards), how
much each payment is, account numbers, and balances. This is very important because the creditor
that is reviewing your application will calculate
your debt-to-income ratio (how much you owe
versus how much you make) to determine what
amount of monthly payment you can afford. If you
owe too much, chances are you'll either be turned
down or you'll receive a conditioned approval. A
conditioned approval could mean that you are
approved for a payment of a certain amount (or
less) but not a penny more, or you might be line
5'd. Line 5'd refers to the total amount financed
on a contract (example: only allowed to finance XX
dollars for XX months). The debt-to-income ratio
has a crucial role in the approval process. The purpose is to keep you from driving through that
valley of financial despair.

> First and
> foremost—
> always tell
> the truth!

5. *References*—Have complete names and addresses
along with phone numbers of three or four personal references of good character. Do not use
someone who is not of good character. It will only
hurt you.

6. *Automotive Insurance*—Know ahead of time from
whom you will get insurance. You will be required
to have it in order to drive off the lot. That's the
law! Have the company name and agent, the
address and phone number, and the policy
number or binder number.

7. *Cosigner*—If your credit is insufficient or you
have had credit problems, you are probably going
to need someone to sign with you on the contract
(unless you are buying under the first-time buyer

or the college grad program). The cosigner must be someone who is willing to be responsible for the loan in case you default (don't make required payments). The cosigner must be established and have good credit or else you're wasting your time and the potential creditor's time.

As you can see, there are many different things that are considered when qualifying a customer for a loan and a tremendous amount of information is needed for the credit application. Be prepared and have it all written down prior to going to the dealership or bank. Financial representatives will respect that from you because it makes everyone's job much easier. It shows that you truly care and that you are putting your best efforts forward.

Payoffs (on Your Trade-In)

If you are trading in an automobile that has been financed and there is a remaining balance owed on the loan, this balance is called a payoff. Call the financial institution where your trade is financed and get your payoff before going to the dealership. Also, find out how long that payoff amount is good for. It could change daily depending on what type of loan you have. If there is credit insurance (life and accidental health) and/or extended warranty added to the loan, these policies should be cancelled the same day that your loan is paid off. Insurance will be prorated based on how long it was in effect. Extended warranties will be prorated based on time (number of months in effect) or mileage (how many miles driven), whichever is more. If the dealer originally handled your loan, then any refunds from these cancellations will be mailed directly to the dealership, and it is their respon-

> Call the financial institution where your trade is financed and get your payoff before going to the dealership.

sibility to forward them to you. These refunds can actually be calculated ahead of time and applied to a payoff balance if you're upside down in your trade. Any down payment (of any kind) will help the equity position and lessen the new auto loan amount financed, therefore making it easier to budget.

While we're on this topic, I want to make you aware of more inside secrets regarding refunds from cancelled credit insurance and extended warranties. When a customer pays a loan off early either by trading to another unit or simply by paying it off in full, the refunds are mailed to the dealer. If these refunds were not allocated for a down payment on a new purchase, the finance and insurance department many times will conveniently and accidentally forget about them as they watch their profit grow and grow!

That is, unless the customer calls and inquires about his or her money. What if customers don't even know they're due a refund? Think they'll ever see it? Not a chance! When these refunds are issued, they are called charge-backs. They are charged back to the finance department profit. This directly affects the finance manager's pay. That, my friends, is why they conveniently and accidentally forget. Millions of dollars in refunds go unclaimed every year. If you plan to trade early or want to pay off your auto early, be sure to ask about cancellation refunds. The finance and insurance department just might forget, and of course you know it would purely be an oversight!

> While we're on this topic, I want to make you aware of more inside secrets regarding refunds from cancelled credit insurance and extended warranties.

The Plan for You

You would be absolutely shocked to know how many customers sign those papers and are totally clueless as to what they just committed themselves to. They are so excited about their new purchase and are so lost in the moment that everything goes in one ear and out the other. They don't know what type of contract they have. They are clueless as to what kind of interest rate they're paying, when their first payment is due, and if there is a grace period (number of days one has to make a payment after due date). They couldn't tell you what their total amount financed is with added tax, tags, title and license, insurance and warranty (if purchased), or what their total of payments will be. All they seem to absorb is how much their monthly payment is, and sometimes they don't know that, even after everything is supposedly disclosed.

An F&I (finance and insurance) manager is required by law to properly disclose all of the particulars to every finance customer at the finalization of the sale, but many will add fuel to the fire and increase the level of excitement causing a major deficiency in concentration. This premeditated effort enables the F&I manager to be rather vague and leave out bits and pieces of the disclosure. The reasoning behind it is to avoid or dodge any unwanted questioning that may lead customers to change their mind about financing arrangements. The dealer could lose a tremendous amount of profit made on interest rates, credit insurance, and extended warranties that the customers are persuaded to buy, or possibly lose the complete deal at both ends (auto and financing). So get unlost in the moment and pay attention! It's very easy to slip a lease contract or a balloon note (example: 35 payments of $250 and one final payment of $4,500) in all that paperwork. It is done all of the time.

As for grace periods, it's much better in the long run to make payments on or before the due date. Grace

periods were ideally designed to help a customer out in the event they are in a money pinch. This allows a little extra time to make the payment or payment arrangements and is not to be misused. If you do misuse grace periods, it could come back to haunt you later on by showing up on your credit report as a continual slow payment pattern, and the next time you apply for credit, you could be charged a higher interest rate or possibly turned down. So make those payments on time! You don't need those high interest rates, okay? Now you have to decide which payment plan best suits your needs.

Conventional

Though leasing is on the rise, the majority of all automotive purchases continue to be financed through conventional methods, the standard installment contracts of thirty-six, forty-eight, or sixty equal payments. After it's paid for, that baby is yours! Occasionally someone will finance for twelve or twenty-four months, but most of us can't afford that high of a monthly obligation. (In thirteen years, I only had two customers finance for twelve months. One was a doctor, and the other one was a young man with newly found wealth—he won the state lottery). Longer terms of seventy-two and eighty-four months are also offered, but as I have already expressed, don't go there! It will cost you an additional fortune on interest alone and talk about being upside down in your trade if you ever decide to get rid of it! If you keep your vehicles for a long time, prefer ownership over renting, or have a tendency to be rough and tough on the wear and tear internally and externally, then conventional financing is recommended.

> Though leasing is on the rise, the majority of all automotive purchases continue to be financed through conventional methods.

Balloon Notes

They're great for someone who prefers ownership but who truly needs smaller monthly payments to fit their budget. This means having one large final payment. Just make sure you understand that when signing the contract. The problem with this plan is that many people do not prepare themselves for that grand finale of a payment, and when it's time to pay up, they have to borrow more money just to make the final payment or refinance the balance. Consequently, they end up paying much more for their vehicle than they originally bargained for. If you choose this plan, prepare for it and save!

First-Time Buyer/College Graduate

There are finance programs available to first-time buyers or college graduates, as discussed in Chapters 5 and 6. The plans are available to anyone who has never financed an automobile before or has recently graduated from college or will be graduating within the academic semester (must have a diploma or some form of written verification). No derogatory (bad) credit can be on your credit file. Most of the automotive finance companies offer these special plans and additional incentives.

Farm

Since farmers depend mostly on their crops for their livelihood, financial lenders have plans available especially for them. Here's an example of a farm plan: For a four-year loan, in the first year there would be eleven small payments of $100 and a twelfth payment of $4,000. The second year would be eleven small payments of $100 and a twelfth payment of $3,500. The third year would be eleven small payments of $100 and a twelfth payment of

> There are finance programs available to first-time buyers or college graduates.

$3,000, and so on and so forth. These plans are more or less custom made to fit each farmer's special circumstances based on the type of farming involved (cattle, dairy, poultry, crops).

I once sold five brand new 4x4 trucks in one day to a crop farmer who had just been in two weeks prior browsing around on the lot. He was trying to figure out a way to buy the new truck he so desperately needed. His old one had finally died. During the two-week period between when he had first been in and when he actually came back to buy, he struck oil on his property! He not only ended up buying a new truck for himself, but for each one of his four sons as well. He financed them using the farm plan and when his oil residuals started oozing in, he paid them off.

Other

With a world full of diversity, there are many financial plans to select from. The automotive world and the finance world work hand in hand on a day-to-day basis to create plans for many different needs. Manufacturing companies, banks, and credit unions all have their own specialties to offer. A lot of these plans are basically the same but are modified to suit individual company preferences and are tagged with their own unique title. One of the more recent trendy plans is actually the old-fashioned second mortgage or equity loan. Every time you turn the TV or radio on, you hear a commercial advertising some wonderful new way to get a loan or buy a car. It doesn't matter what your credit is, how much money you have for a down payment, or how much you owe. If you own a home, you're approved.

I don't believe it's a good idea to borrow against your home because there are much better choices. Before you

> Farmers can be broke one day and a week later be rich as a "tractor trailer full of cattle or chickens," "a wagon load of tobacco," or "harvested wheat fields."

know it, you end up owing a fortune, and eventually the payment consumes your total paycheck. What if you have to move for some reason? Will you be able to get as much as you owe for your home? Are you settled and will you live there the rest of your life or are you just starting out? These points must be taken into consideration.

It sounds so easy. Pay off all of your credit cards, buy a new car, or consolidate your bills and lump it all together. Do you want to pay on a car loan for thirty years? Before signing anything, be absolutely certain that you have reviewed all of your options and have chosen the best possible plan for your specific needs. Work with your budget, not against it, and look at the long-term picture!

Cobuyer/Cosigner

Both of these will sign on a loan with the principle buyer (the main buyer), but they are not to be confused. The cobuyer is partial owner or co-owner of the property being purchased and is equally responsible for all payments. Both names will appear on the title. The cosigner is not owner of the property being purchased but is assisting the principle buyer in getting a loan by lending his or her good credit status. Only the principle buyer's name will appear on the title. Should the principle buyer fail to make timely payments, the financial institution will look to the cosigner for payment.

Since the loan involves more than one person in either case, you must be extremely careful not to go over your budget. If you decide to add any credit insurance or extended warranty on your loan, the other person must be in total agreement with this decision. As you know, the payments become higher with this added protection. If you fail to make timely payments and your account

> The cobuyer is partial owner or co-owner of the property being purchased and is equally responsible for all payments. Both names will appear on the title.

becomes delinquent, it will not only reflect on your credit, but will reflect on the cobuyer's or cosigner's credit as well. And that would not be pretty!

For those of you who are unable to find a cobuyer/cosigner and get the bright idea of forging the name of someone, don't even think about it. This is fraud and you are asking for serious trouble.

I had a customer that bought a Maxima Wagon for his new business. Due to the amount of the loan and the lack of credit established by his business, he needed a strong cosigner. The next day I received a phone call from his father (we thought). He gave me all of his credit information. Because they lived almost seventy miles away, his father was unable to make the trip. (Supposedly his health was really bad and he couldn't travel.) Anyway, being the anxious salespeople that we were, we were eager to get the loan approved, which we did. Then it was time to sign the papers! Having convinced all of us at the dealership how bad off his father was physically, we decided to go ahead and deliver the car to him in good faith. However, he would have to get every form notarized by a notary public with two witnesses.

The customer took the forms home and then brought them all back in a timely fashion, signed and notarized as requested. Everybody was happy. He got what he wanted and we got what we wanted. Three months later, I received a phone call from the lender through which the Maxima was financed. This guy hadn't made a single payment on it and they were trying to locate him in order to repossess the car. All of his phone numbers had been disconnected and he had moved. I also received a phone call from his enraged father, who just happened to not know a thing about cosigning for any car loan. The lender had started harassing him for payment.

This man was not only furious but crushed as well. His own son, his own flesh and blood, had used him, forged his name, and caused him a tremendous amount of trouble and heartache. As it turned out, the original call from the customer's father was obviously not from his father. The notary, the witnesses, everything, were all faked. I had even called the notary office to verify the legitimacy of it and that was faked. With the father's help, the lender located the son, retrieved the vehicle, and charges were brought against him.

The dealership was certainly in jeopardy because the rules had been bent on the sale and delivery of the vehicle, but salespeople are eager beavers and are prone to presuming people are honest once in a while. I must say though, I never repeated this mistake again! Eventually the charges were dropped because it was a family affair, but the father-son relationship was ruined.

Cash Down

If you are going to finance your purchase, you are far better off to save your money until you have enough to make a substantial down payment. I'm not talking about the manufacturer rebates. I'm talking about cash money straight from your own pocket. Those of you who have very little or no credit, or who have had credit problems in the past, are definitely going to need a larger down payment. The lenders will require it. Those of you who are clean as a whistle will not need as much, but the fact remains: The more down payment you have the lower your payment will be. So save that money to get those payments down!

Credit Problems

Have you had problems making payments on time, had collections, liens, or judgements filed against you? Have you had property repossessed or filed for bankruptcy? Not to be insensitive to your feelings whatsoever, but ALRIGHT ALREADY! You've crashed and burned. What are you gonna do about it? We all have our share of problems and hard times, but as cold as it may seem and no matter what happened or whose fault it was, dealers and lenders aren't really interested in hearing your sob stories. All they know is that your credit report is bad and that you are a high risk. You obviously can't go back in time and change things. What's done is done. What you *can* do is reach for that silver lining high in the sky and change your future.

These days there are many second-chance opportunities available to people with bad credit. As with mortgage and equity loans, every time you turn the radio on, watch TV, or open the newspaper, in great big bold colorful print there's a dealer advertising special financing just for you. So get out of the ditch and get back on the road again. If you meet all of the qualifications such as length of residency, adequate time on the job, have adequate verifiable income, have a home phone, etc., you can get approved.

For those who have filed bankruptcy, you will need to provide a copy of your discharge letter from the court (a letter stating that your bankruptcy case has been discharged). Face it though, if this shoe fits, it's going to be expensive! Be prepared to pay higher prices, higher interest rates, heftier down payments, and depending on your particular situation, you may even need a cosigner. One other thing—you may not get the vehicle of your choice, but you'll get something.

Regardless of who it is, don't ever forge anything for any reason. Not only will you get caught (if not immediately, somewhere down the road), but it just isn't worth all the aggravation, heartache, or time behind bars.

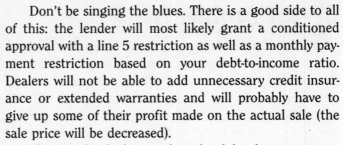

"You can't always get what you want!"

Don't be singing the blues. There is a good side to all of this: the lender will most likely grant a conditioned approval with a line 5 restriction as well as a monthly payment restriction based on your debt-to-income ratio. Dealers will not be able to add unnecessary credit insurance or extended warranties and will probably have to give up some of their profit made on the actual sale (the sale price will be decreased).

That is why dealers push so hard for down payment. The bigger your down payment is, the more profit they can squeeze into these restricted deals. Cry pauper until you know for sure just exactly how much of a down payment you actually have to come up with. Hold out and don't give in. Tell them you are limited on how much down payment you have, if any at all. Make them dig into *their* pocket! One thing is for sure: With a restricted deal, your budget will be kept in line, and that's what we want!

CHAPTER 8

Leasing

I n our society, with the retail world being what it is, prices on everything continue to increase on a daily basis and as a result, it's becoming a real hardship for many to buy new transportation. That's why leasing is flourishing more than ever. Dealers, being the venomous scorpions that they are, will take advantage of distraught customers and convince them that they can lease the vehicle of their dreams with less down stroke and still have cheaper monthly payments than when purchasing.

With an appealing ring to it, customers blindly give the go-ahead, not fully comprehending the lease except that the payments are cheaper. The dealer will then turn on the old charm, "Well for only forty dollars more a month, you can drive that special car you've always wanted!"

Come on now—why don't they just dangle a bunch of carrots in front of Bugs Bunny, for crying out loud! A customer can quickly get distracted and lose sight of his or her budget. What does the dealer get out of this? More sales and more money. The more expensive the unit, the more profitable it can be for the dealer.

Before we go any further, let's make sure that everyone is on the same page. Take a few moments to study the following terms. An understanding of the whole concept of leasing will come much easier if you do.

Leasing is the sure way to budget, or at least that's what the automotive industry would have you believe.

The Language of Leasing

Capitalized (Cap) Cost The best straight-out (no trade) purchase price.

Gross Capitalized Cost The best straight-out (no trade) purchase price, plus any additional items you pay for over the lease term (such as extended warranties, insurance, and any outstanding prior credit or lease balance).

Capitalized Cost Reduction The down payment (cash, net trade-in/trade-in minus payoff, manufacturer rebates, and dealer incentives) that is deducted from the capitalized cost.

Net Capitalized Cost Gross capitalized cost minus capitalized cost reduction.

Acquisition Fee Up-front dealer or lender charges for processing and handling a lease. The fee is set by the individual lender.

Disposition Fee Lease-end dealer or lender charges made for the disposal of a leased unit. The individual lender determines the fee.

Security Deposit Up-front deposit required, usually equal to the monthly lease payment rounded to the next twenty-five dollar increment (example: lease payment = $244.26, security deposit = $250).

Residual Value Estimated or projected value of a vehicle at the end of a lease determined by the individual lender.

Depreciation The value lost by a leased unit throughout the lease. It is also described as the difference between the net capitalized cost and the residual value.

Money Factor The lease rate (comparable to the finance rate) determined by the lender. To figure out what the rate charge is, simply multiply the money cost factor (a five-figured decimal) by 2,400.

Gap Protection Insurance on a lease to cover the gap between what an individual's auto insurance would pay and what the lease buyout would be (including early termination penalties) if a leased unit is totaled, stolen, or has physical damage prior to lease end. Gap insurance can also be available on standard financing. Ask your insurance agent for details.

Closed-End Lease This is a lease in which customers have two options:

1. At lease end, they can turn the leased vehicle back in and lease another one or walk away free and clear provided there are no penalty charges (excess mileage or excess wear and tear).
2. They can purchase the leased vehicle for the estimated residual value stated in their lease contract. A word of advice on purchasing your lease: Only purchase it if the value is the same as or less than the estimated residual value. You can sell it privately for a profit and then buy or lease a new one.

Purchase Option Fee A fee paid along with the residual value in the event a customer decides to purchase their lease. The individual lender sets the fee.

Open-End Lease This is a lease in which customers have two options:

1. At lease end, they can turn the leased vehicle back in but must pay any difference in the actual

current residual value and the estimated residual value stated in their lease contract plus any and all penalties for excess wear and tear and excess mileage.

2. They can purchase the leased vehicle for the actual current residual value.

These are bad news! Don't even consider an open-end lease! It could cost you several thousands.

Excess Mileage Charge A charge for any additional mileage driven in excess of the annual mileage allowance. The amount of the charge will usually vary from 10–25 cents per mile depending on the lender's policy.

Normal and Excess Wear and Tear This usually refers to maintenance, soiling, dents, scratches, chipped paint, rusted areas, broken and/or missing parts including bulbs, upholstery tears or burns, brakes, tires, etc.) Before signing any contract, make sure the normal and excess wear and tear clause has been accurately disclosed to you verbally and is a part of the lease contract. What you consider to be normal wear and tear could be different than what the dealer and/or the lessor considers normal wear and tear. Major penalties for excess wear and tear can quickly add up. The safest and most economical way to drive a leased vehicle is to take extremely good care of it and do not drive over the annual mileage allowance. High mileage wears on the value fast.

Early Termination Ending the lease early. Warning, warning; more major penalties! It will cost you major money!

Base Monthly Payment The monthly lease payment including rate charge without usage (sales) tax.

Total of Base Monthly Payments The depreciation plus the rate charge.

Total Monthly Payment The monthly lease payment including rate charge with usage (sales) tax.

Lease A contracted agreement between a lender (lessor) and a customer (lessee) in which the lessee pays for the usage of a vehicle owned by the lessor over a period of time.

Lessor A lender who buys vehicles from a dealer and leases them to a customer. Sometimes dealers will have their own in-house lease program. In that case the dealer is the lessor.

Lessee The customer that leases a unit from a lender or dealer. Remember that the lessee does not own the leased vehicle. The lessor owns it and the lessee uses it.

Monthly Usage Tax Sales tax that is paid on each base monthly payment versus all the taxes being paid up front at time of purchase.

Lease Term The number of months in a lease.

Regulation M Effective January 1, 1998, Regulation M of the *Federal Consumer Leasing Act Disclosures* is the new federal law requiring dealers and lenders to fully disclose all costs of a lease. In the past, dealers and lenders were not required to disclose all costs.

Ending the lease early. Warning, warning; more major penalties! It will cost you major money!

> A lease can be negotiated just like a purchase!

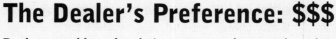

The Dealer's Preference: $$$

Dealers would prefer their customers lease rather than buy, and here's why:

1. Leasing is extremely profitable. Because so many customers do not understand leasing in its entirety, it is a very easy and effortless way for dealers to attain enormous amounts of profit, and they do! The uninformed customers do not realize that a lease can be negotiated. Yes, you read it right!

   These uninformed customers blindly accept any lease without any resistance whatsoever, thus getting blatantly ripped off. *DON'T EVER WALK INTO A SHOWROOM AND TELL A DEALER THAT YOU WANT TO LEASE AN AUTOMOBILE UNTIL AFTER YOU HAVE NEGOTIATED AND AGREED UPON A STRAIGHT-OUT (NO-TRADE) PURCHASE PRICE (AS IF YOU WERE GOING TO BUY IT).* Even if you are responding to some unbelievably great ad you saw or heard, negotiate a best no-trade purchase price first. (There's probably a catch to that great ad.) Then and only then do you mention leasing. If you are looking at a new unit and you don't negotiate first, the dealer could lease the automobile to you at full sticker price plus 100 percent or more of the MSRP. A dealer could markup your lease 110–115 percent of the MSRP depending on the lender guidelines and you'd never know unless you were familiar with leasing terms and knew what to watch for. The highest I ever leased a vehicle to a customer for was at 115 percent of MSRP and was I ever happy.

Here's an example: Let's say that Heather, our beloved sales representative, has convinced Elizabeth to lease her new car instead of buying it. If you'll recall, the MSRP was $16,485. If Heather leases the car to Elizabeth for full sticker price, she has made $1,978.20 in profit, plus holdback and whatever rebates and additional incentives there might be. Now, if Heather marks the lease up to 115 percent of MSRP, which would be $18,957.75, that is an additional profit of $2,472.75. Add them together and the total profit would be $4,450.95 plus the extras. Now let's be specific and say there is a $1,500 customer rebate on the particular car that Elizabeth is leasing. Add that to the total and now the grand total profit is $5,950.95. And again, don't forget the holdback and additional dealer incentives that are added to the grand total profit. Leasing can be another form of highway robbery if you're not careful. This goes for used merchandise as well. A used automobile can just as easily be marked up. If you're leasing a used car, make sure you have done your homework and know its retail and wholesale value before agreeing to any price or signing any lease. With Regulation M in effect, the outrageously jacked up prices on leasing should soon dwindle away. It's up to you to stop it though! It's up to you to negotiate that price down!

2. The more customers a dealer can convince to lease, the fewer charge-backs there will be, therefore keeping all of their profit in pocket. If a lessee tries to terminate a lease early, there will be steep early termination penalties to pay along with the balance of the lease. Once customers sign a lease, they are locked in for the total

Dealers would prefer their customers lease rather than buy, and here's why.

amount, and the only way to get out of it is to pay those painful penalties. Dealers and finance/lease managers love that!

3. One sure way of keeping customers coming back for more is to sell them on a lease. A lease will bring customers back into the showroom quicker than a purchase will. With a closed-end lease, customers must return their leased unit and either purchase it for the estimated residual value, turn it in and lease or buy another one, (an opportunity for the dealer to make yet another sale and more profit), or simply walk away—after paying all penalties, of course.

Open-end leases are highway robbery. If offered one, vamoose quickly. As far as where to return a leased unit, any authorized dealer can accept one. In fact, they invite them because there is such a big demand for good quality used automobiles. If a lease is an in-house lease through the actual dealer, then the unit will probably have to be returned there. Play it safe, though, and always ask. Rules will vary from company to company. Whatever the case may be, special arrangements can always be made in the event someone moves or is transferred.

Comparative Breakdown

Now that you have studied the lease terminology and have gotten familiar with it, let's do a comparative breakdown on leasing versus buying and see just how leasing actually works. Leasing information is listed on the left side and buying information is listed on the right side.

LEASING

Capitalized (Cap) Cost
+ Extended Warranties, Insurance,
   Payoff or Lease Balance

Gross Capitalized Cost

Gross Capitalized Cost
– Capitalized Cost Reduction

Net Capitalized Cost

Net Capitalized Cost
(does not include Sales Tax, Title, and License)
– Estimated Residual Value

Depreciation

Depreciation
+ Rate Charge

Total Base Monthly Payments

$$\frac{\text{Total Base Monthly Payments}}{\text{Lease Term}} = \text{Base Monthly Payment}$$

Base Monthly Payment
+ Monthly Usage Tax (sales tax)

Total Monthly Payment

BUYING

Best No-Trade Price
+ Sales Tax, Title, and License

Total Best No-Trade Price

Total Best No-Trade Price
– Down Payment

Unpaid Balance

Unpaid Balance
+ Payoff, Extended Warranty,
   Credit Insurance, and Fees

Amount Financed

Amount Financed
+ Finance Charge

Total of Payments

When buying, the payments are figured on the total unpaid balance, which includes sales tax, tags, title, license, extended warranties, credit insurance, and any outstanding prior credit or lease balance plus calculated interest. When leasing, payments are figured quite differently. The net (adjusted) capitalized cost (which does not include sales tax, tags, title, or license) minus the estimated residual value equals the depreciation. Now add the rate charge (calculated by multiplying the money factor/lease rate by 2,400) to the depreciation, and you come up with the total of base monthly payments. Divide the total of base monthly payments by the lease term (number of months) and that will equal the base monthly payment.

You must pay monthly usage tax (sales tax) on the base monthly payment. The percentage depends on the state you live in. Once you have figured out what the monthly usage tax will be, add that to the base monthly payment, and, finally, you have your total monthly payment! This sounds complicated, but figuring lease payments is very simple if you know these things:

- Capitalized cost (your best straight-out, no-trade purchase price)
- Capitalized cost reduction (down payment)
- Estimated residual value
- Lease charge

Remember, extended warranties, credit insurance, and any outstanding prior credit or lease balances are added to the capitalized cost and becomes the gross capitalized cost. All of these extras make the lease payment higher.

Additional Fees and Penalties

If you will review the lease definitions for a moment, you'll see that there are several different fees and possible penalties that could turn what you thought to be a cheaper route into an overall very costly experience.

The up-front costs alone would make a really nice down payment towards a purchase. Penalties? Well that's another story. The percentage of returned leased units that are in 100 percent acceptable condition as far as wear and tear is extremely small. It's your opinion versus the dealer's opinion, and they almost always find something wrong, which means you pay up!

As for the mileage, most people end up driving over their mileage allowance, costing themselves even more money. So think about it. Look at the whole picture. How much above and beyond your lease payments is your dream car really going to cost you to drive (not own)? And, might I add, you are still responsible for all maintenance and must carry full coverage insurance.

Without all the additional expenses, leasing would be a great way to drive, but you can't get rid of them.

Amounts Due at Lease Signing and Delivery

Here is an itemization of the amounts due at a lease signing or delivery. In 1, I'm not referring to rebates, dealer incentives, or non-cash discounts, but to the customer's actual out-of-pocket cash down payment.

How much is that Mercedes in the window?

1. Capitalized cost reduction (out-of-pocket cash down payment)
2. First monthly payment (sometimes two payments are required, depending on the lender)

> When you sign a lease you do not own the vehicle.

3. Refundable security deposit (More times than not, the security deposit is not refunded, but rather applied to the penalty charges.)
4. Title fees
5. Registration fees
6. Sales tax (on the out-of-pocket cash down payment)
7. Acquisition fee

Add this all up and it comes to a lot of money! It's money that you are giving away because you're not buying the vehicle but just using it.

The dealer assigns (transfers) the lease to the lender and the lender buys your vehicle making the lender the owner. You are paying rent every month to the lender for the privilege of driving it. The vehicle will be registered in your name, but the title will have the lender's name on it. So if you do decide to lease, don't pay any more cash down than you have to because it's not your ride, plus the less up-front down payment you make, the smaller the amount of taxes you'll have to pay.

There are a few other costs not included in the amount due upon signing and delivery but that are definitely in the contract. One is the gap protection, which is or can be included in your lease depending on the lender. This covers the gap between what an individual's auto insurance would pay and what the lease buyout would be (including early termination penalties) if a leased unit is totaled, stolen, or has physical damage prior to lease end.

Another cost is the disposition fee. This is paid at the end of a lease for the return of a vehicle if the customer does not purchase it. Like the acquisition fee, it will range in price depending on the lender. Still another cost is the purchase option fee, which is charged if a customer decides to purchase his or her leased unit. And again the fee will vary. As if these aren't enough, there may very well be even more fees depending on the lender.

In addition, you've got penalty charges to consider. Here's where a lease can really turn sour.

> Fees, fees, and more fees!

Penalties

1. **Residual** This is an estimated or projected value. If you don't purchase the leased unit, you will have to pay for any difference in the actual value and what was estimated. And like I said, there's almost always a difference. I don't recall very many customers that didn't have to pay out something!

2. **Excess Mileage Charge** This one will really sneak up on you before you know it. It's very hard to restrict your driving to a minimal amount, especially if you have kids. Our world simply moves too fast!

3. **Excess Wear and Tear** All I've got to say is that you better treat your leased vehicle like a newborn baby for the whole term of the lease. Your idea of wear and tear and the dealer or lender's idea of wear and tear can be worlds apart!

4. **Early Termination** There is no advantage to terminating a lease. You still have to pay the remaining balance of unpaid lease payments plus early termination penalties plus any excessive mileage plus excessive wear and tear. Basically, it's plus, plus, plus.

5. **Open-End Lease** NO! NO! NO! An open-end lease will cost you every time because there is no locked-in, guaranteed residual value at the end of the lease term. You are responsible for any and all difference, and there is always a difference.

Early termination penalties, excess wear and tear penalties, and excess mileage penalties could cost you thousands of dollars.

Final Overview

With all of the detailed, easy-to-comprehend information in this chapter, you should be able to make not only an educated decision, but also the right decision on whether leasing or financing is your best option. As you can see, besides the monthly lease payments, there are many other charges to consider. Review this chapter several times and think long and hard before signing a lease.

Once you've signed on that dotted line, you are not only responsible for the full balance, but you are locked in for the full term. You can't just up and trade when you want to, and if you're planning on having any kind of social life at all or taking any trips, you'd better buy or rent another vehicle. Mileage adds up quickly.

That's a lot of money to be shelling out on something that doesn't belong to you. You might ask yourself: Will I benefit any from a lease? Maybe, if it's for a business and you can utilize it somehow when filing taxes or if you always trade every year or two. You might get to drive a more expensive car for a while, but you're still throwing a lot of money away. Are you truly a lease candidate? Ask yourself if leasing is your best way to budget.

CHAPTER 9

The Finance and Insurance Department as a Profit Center

And the Finance Manager said to the Sales Manager, "Let's just see how much blood we can squeeze out of this one on the back end (the financing) since he didn't give us what we wanted on the front end (the sale of the vehicle)." Are you surprised? By now you shouldn't be! No matter how heartless and cold it sounds, that's exactly what they say, that's exactly how they think, and that's exactly what the boss expects them to do. It's their job, remember? For every penny they lose on the front end, they will kill to make it up on the back end.

If you don't give them what they want, they team up on you like some street gang with the finance manager on one side and the sales team on the other. Talk about pressure! It's a mighty cruel world out there, so the sooner you toughen up, the better off you'll be. The more you resist, the harder they attack.

By the time a customer is ready to enter the finance office, the dealer's plan of attack has already been implemented. For example, if you wanted to pay cash, the sales team would ask you not once, but several times if you would rather finance and save your hard earned cash for future investments

It's called the Power of Persuasion. It's in the best interest of the finance manager and the sales manager to work together because without sales there is no financing, and without financing there are few sales. Together they are dangerous!

and upcoming opportunities? And then they go into this long explanation as to why you should and how much money you will save.

If you wanted to finance through your own personal sources, the sales team would mention repeatedly what a terrific finance program they have and that they could beat your rates. They would also ask if you would rather finance your major purchases elsewhere and save your personal bank or credit union for the more personal needs and emergencies? Why all of this persuasion? They are trying to change your direction in order to make more money. Oh, and they absolutely cannot forget to tell you about the wonderful extended warranty plans that are available.

All of this is an attempt to make more money! It is the sales team's job to plant seeds of diversion in order to help the F&I manager. They will attempt to convert you from your original purchase plan, and will prep you so the F&I manager can do his deed, sell you a bag of goods, or as I called it earlier, laha, croak, and choke. This bag of goodies contains F&I products (life and accidental health insurance, warranties, etc.).

You've completed the sales portion and negotiated your best purchase price and now you're ready to walk into the finance (business) office, and almost immediately you're under attack. You don't realize it because these guys are such smooth operators and they really know how to lay down their lines!

In fact, they have all the right lines memorized for every type of customer there is. They've got lines for every single objection you could imagine and they know exactly when and how to use them. They're schooled and rehearsed. Actually, both finance and sales personnel are schooled and rehearsed. They not only receive training on the job, but they are required to attend schools, classes, seminars, meetings, and conferences. This keeps them up-to-date on all of the newest product information and the latest sales techniques and sales tools—everything needed to be successful in the automotive industry. If it's offered, they go.

I received extensive training in finance and insurance/leasing and sales at a school in Chicago when I first began. I attended many other training sessions throughout my thirteen years in the business. You wouldn't believe all the material I had to memorize. There are scripts for converting cash, bank, and credit union customers to persuade them to finance through the dealership in order to maximize profit. There are scripts for selling credit life and accidental health insurance and extended warranties (at huge profits). If you have ever been through the buying or financing process at a dealership, you are already familiar with what I'm talking about. Sales teams and finance managers will fill your head with all of the reasons why you should finance with them and why you should buy their bag of goods. They won't give up until you either say yes or until they have visibly pushed you too far, making you angry. They know that eventually some of us suckers will give in. That's the plan. It is the power of persuasion! But do you really need all this laha, croak, and choke?

> Hmmm, how sweet it is, the power of persuasion! Mo' money! Mo' money! Mo' money! Mo' money! Mo' money! Mo' money!

Credit Insurance: Yes or No?
Life Insurance

It would be wonderful to live forever and never grow old but that just isn't The Almighty's plan. At least it isn't here on earth. We are born into our physical bodies and

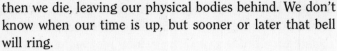

They know that eventually some of us "SUCKERS" will give in.

then we die, leaving our physical bodies behind. We don't know when our time is up, but sooner or later that bell will ring.

As a responsible person, we should do as much as we can to prepare for this eventuality, and buying life insurance should certainly be considered at least for the amount of debt we have, especially if we are married or have a family. It's better to have it and not need it than not to have it and need it.

If you have any debt whatsoever like mortgage payments, car payments, personal and school loans, credit cards, etc., who's going to pay for those debts if something happens to you? Your survivors—that's who. That is why you need life insurance so that in the event of your death, if you have enough coverage, not only will all of your burial expenses be paid, but all of your debts will be paid as well. If you don't have enough or don't have any at all, somebody will be held responsible for paying those bills. Whether it's your spouse, your family, your estate, or a cosigner, lenders and bill collectors will collect and they don't care where it comes from either!

Do you want to leave your loved ones with this burden, especially after they suffer your loss? There's a line, but how true it is. This is one of many that you will hear in the finance office except theirs will be much more dramatic and morbid.

If you are financing an automobile, whom should you buy this coverage through? The lender (the dealer or the bank you finance through)? Your credit union? Many times they offer it free of charge! This one's a no-brainer— of course you're going to accept it if it's free. Your own personal insurance agent? Do you want to cover only the balance of your auto loan, or do you want to cover all of your debts? Credit insurance through a lender will pay off only one debt: the auto loan. Insurance through your agent can pay off all your debts depending on the amount of coverage you choose. The credit insurance that lenders offer is overpriced but there are usually no physicals or blood work needed since the insurance sold is most likely a group plan. You can get a level term policy through your own insurance agent, and I guarantee the cost will be much cheaper.

However, if you have any pre-existing ailments, it may be more difficult for you to get coverage since a physical and blood work may be needed. What makes more sense: a higher premium through the dealer/lender for less coverage or a lower premium through your personal insurance agent with more coverage?

Here's why lender premiums are so high. An agreement is made with an insurance company to sell their insurance, and in return the dealer/lender keeps a percentage of the premium charged on each policy sold. The largest percentage I ever retained was 65 percent. There are two types of credit insurance on loans: single and joint. Single is for one person and joint is for two people. Let's say you give in and buy life insurance on your loan (joint coverage for you and your cosigner) and the premium is $1,000. The agreement between the dealer and the insurance company is 65 percent to the dealer and 35 percent to the insurance company. That's $650 in profit ($1,000 x 65% = $650). Now deduct the $650 from the $1,000 premium you were charged and that leaves a balance of $350. That portion goes to the insurance company.

You could have gone to your own personal agent and gotten the same coverage for much less. Now are you shocked? You should be! You probably do need life insurance depending on your personal circumstances, but not through car dealers and lenders with outrageously priced

> They want to fill your conscience with guilt and scare you "to death" so you'll buy.

A truly "bit-
tersweet"
victory
turned
tragedy . . .

premiums. The most economical way to buy insurance is through an agent (coverage that would pay off all of your debts). Base the amount on how much you owe and/or how much you would want to leave your loved ones in the event your bell tolls.

I'll never, ever forget the first credit life policy I sold. I had just gotten back from F&I (finance and insurance) school and was I ever pumped up. That's an understatement! I could have sold meat to the strictest vegetarians. There I was, a full-fledged, certified F&I manager, just waiting for my first victim to sell dealer financing, credit life, accidental health, and extended warranty. So here they come floating on cloud nine, Joyce and Tom, all proud of their brand new Monte Carlo, Tom's favorite car. Well, I did it! I convinced them to finance with us instead of going to their bank. I sold them joint credit life insurance and a major extended warranty. Now I was the one floating on cloud nine, more like cloud one hundred. My first finance sale, my first F&I protection, and my first extended warranty. The total profit was a little over $3,000. This was in 1983 so $3,000 was quite a lot of profit.

Anyway, Tom and Joyce took delivery of their newly financed car and were on their merry way. Day after day business went on as usual and I improved with each customer at selling goods. Then, exactly six weeks after purchase date, Tom had a massive heart attack and died. I can't begin to tell you how I felt. Pain and sadness for Joyce, embarrassment from making such a home run on them and aggravation because every penny I had made in profit was charged back. My eyes had been quickly opened to the harsh reality of "rich today, broke tomorrow." But even worse, I learned the heartbreaking reality of what life insurance is all about: death.

Accidental/Health Insurance

Like life insurance, everyone should have accidental/health insurance if there is any debt. For those of you who don't know what accidental health insurance is, it is insurance that covers your payments in the event you were to get sick, hurt, or disabled for a period of time. The insurance will make your car payments for as long as you are off of work or until you return to work. There are different plans, the 7-14-30 day and the 7-14-30 day retro. On the 7-14-30 day, after the number of required days have passed, the insurance covers from the 8th, 15th, or 31st day forward. The 7-14-30 day retro still refers to the number of days passed but the insurance company will go back to the very first day of missed work and cover the entire period you are unable to work. It is required that one must provide a written doctor's statement monthly verifying the illness, injury, or disability.

You think life insurance is expensive, you ain't seen nothin' yet!

The exact same hounding approach is used when selling accidental health insurance but with a different set of lines. One of them will sound similar to this: "Your payments as well as your credit will be totally protected because if you get sick, hurt, or disabled for a period of days (whatever plan you choose), your payments will be made for you as long as you are off of work. You don't have to worry about them." Here's another one: "You'll have total peace of mind knowing you'll be covered if you are sick, hurt, or disabled." This is great coverage but once again, not through the dealer/lender.

Here's an example of how much a dealer would make off of accidental health insurance. Say you bought life insurance and now the finance manager has persuaded you to buy accidental health insurance at a cost of $1,600. How much of that do you think is profit? Using the same formula as with life insurance, take $1,600 x 65% = $1,040 profit. Deduct $1,040 from the $1,600 premium you were charged and that leaves a balance of $560 which goes to the insurance company. And you know the rest. You could have gone a much cheaper route! On life and accidental health insurance alone the dealer picked up an additional $1,690 profit. That doesn't include the profit made on the actual sale, the profit made on interest rate (dealer reserve), or the profit made on extended warranty.

One Friday afternoon, we were having a huge tent sale. We were totally swamped with customers and didn't have enough sales staff so I was wearing both hats (working sales and finance). One of my customers, Jeffrey, bought a Dodge Stealth at full sticker price because it was a really hot car at the time. I also sold him the aftermarket package (undercoating, fabric protection, and paint sealant). Then it was time to finance and did I ever load him up.

He sunk big time, buying everything (life, accidental health, and extended warranty). I scored all the way around: the car, the aftermarket products, and the finance products. As I recall, the profit on this particular deal was near $6,000. Jeff's payment was very high but he didn't care. He wanted that car no matter how much it cost him. It was his dream car. He took delivery and was gone faster than bullets. Two weeks went by and I received a very distraught phone call from Jeff's sister.

He was a truck driver and had been in a terrible accident. He was laid up in the hospital busted from one end of his body to another and was going to be there for a long time. I thought to myself, "Thank God he had the accidental health insurance." The insurance made his monthly payment for him until he was able to return to work full time. In this case, he was lucky. Though his payments were made for him, he paid a fortune for the coverage and possibly could have gotten it for much less through an independent agent. Don't pay high prices when you can get it for less. Insurance is always good to have, especially when you need it! But at the dealers high price? I don't think so!

If you're going to buy credit insurance, spend the money wisely and go through your personal agent where all of your debts can be paid, not just your auto loan. As for accidental health insurance, it may be tougher to get because of exclusions and pre-existing condition clauses. Check with your personal agent anyway. They might have a plan available that pays out an attractive monthly sum based on how much coverage you buy. Or they might be able to lead you in the right direction to a company that can help you. Whatever you decide, go through an agent you can trust, and as always, shop!

> Prices and the types of insurance available also vary with insurance companies and the particular state you live in.

Extended Warranties (Service Contracts)

There are several questions you should ask yourself to determine whether or not you're a good candidate for an extended warranty. How long are you going to keep your vehicle? Is it leased? How many miles do you drive annually? Do you travel long distances often (vacations, business, etc.)? Do you take extra good care of your vehicle or do you have a tendency to neglect it, including the required general maintenance? Be honest! What type of warranty do you have, if any? These are all very important factors on which to base your decision. If your choice is a new car and you trade frequently (every two or three years), then you are probably not a good candidate.

All new automobiles come with a full factory warranty so why would you even consider buying an extended warranty? Chances are there will still be some remaining factory warranty left when you trade again. You would be wasting your money. The same goes for a lease customer. If your lease is for a term of thirty-six months, you really don't need an extended warranty. You're limited on your mileage anyway so that's not a problem. On a new unit, buy an extended warranty only if you are going to keep it longer than three years and/or drive very high mileage.

If your choice is a used automobile, then we have a different story. I would only consider buying an extended warranty on a used automobile that has no warranty or very little warranty. Remember that many certified used cars have a full warranty provided by the manufacturer or dealer. Some of the program units still have a considerable amount of factory warranty remaining. Perhaps you might luck out and buy one that already has an existing extended warranty that is transferable for a fee.

Once again, if you are going to keep your car for a long time and/or drive high mileage then I would consider an extended warranty. The cost of labor alone is very expensive, and if your repair is anything major, you had best be prepared to lay out *mucho dinero*.

If all of your factory warranty or dealer warranty is expired and you're out traveling away from home somewhere on vacation or business, an extended warranty might be a good thing to have if you break down. Talk about a hefty bill! You don't want to get caught in that situation! Repair shops of all kinds are notorious for taking advantage of broken down travelers. If you've got warranty coverage, you're saved, maybe! If not, then brace yourself. You're up the creek without a paddle. It's a gamble. Regardless of whether you drive a new or used vehicle, if you neglect

Once again, if you are going to keep your car for a long time and/or drive high mileage then I would consider an extended warranty.

your automobile and do not maintain it properly on a regular basis, fulfilling all of the maintenance requirements, no warranty is going to cover your problems.

It doesn't matter how long you keep it, how many miles you drive, or whether you're traveling short or long distances, you must read your owners manual and follow the suggested maintenance requirements!

Karen, a customer of mine, came in early one morning riding with a friend of hers. Right behind them was a tow truck pulling her car. She had been driving down the highway on her way to work when all of a sudden the car just died. She managed to coast over to the side of the road before the car completely stopped rolling. Again and again, Karen tried to restart it but the engine would not fire up. It wouldn't even turn over. Luckily she was close to an exit ramp and was able to walk to a nearby telephone booth. Karen called her friend to come pick her up and called the towing company to come tow her car. Once it was ready, they were on their way to the dealership. The driver of the tow truck pulled the car into the service department where it could be looked at. The service department manager opened the hood and found a blown engine. (She had driven 11,000 miles since her last oil change.)

He wrote up an estimate of what it would cost to repair the car and gave it to Karen. When she saw how much it was going to cost, she decided to trade it in for whatever she could get out of it. (What good is a car with a blown engine? No good at all, if you don't have the money to fix it.) I must tell you that Karen had somewhat of a history of car neglect and everybody knew it.

Anyway, before the day was over she had bought a used car and drove it home that evening. She financed it through the dealership, buying all of the finance products

> Ain't no warranty gonna cover it if you don't fulfill maintenance requirements!

(credit life, accidental health insurance, and extended warranty with comprehensive coverage). I charged her $1,000 over dealer cost for the extra warranty. What can I say, she was an extremely easy and gullible target. Karen had just blown an engine and was broken down on the side of the highway (a situation no woman ever wants or needs to be in).

She certainly didn't want that to happen again, and with the incident fresh on her mind, I was able to dig deep down into her pocket. Sorry, but it's the truth. I had the "Greenback Fever," my own little term for money hungry people). I did, however, stress to her the importance of taking care of one's car and maintaining it regularly according to the maintenance guide. About ten months later I received a phone call from her.

Karen was out in Los Angeles, California, on vacation and broken down again with the same problem—the engine. She called me from her hotel room crying her eyes out and complaining that the extended warranty she had bought was worthless. The company was not going to cover the repairs. As soon as I was able to calm her down, I assured her that I would make some phone calls to the garage where her car was and also to the extended warranty company to try to get some answers. I spoke with the garage owner and he told me that engine was not blown, but there were some serious problems going on due to, once again, maintenance neglect. He said that there was hardly any oil at all in the car and that what little oil there was smelled burned and was so thick and sludgy that it looked like mud. (Honestly, I wasn't surprised. I had wondered how long it would be before something happened.)

I called the warranty company and tried like crazy to get the repairs covered but they simply wouldn't budge. It was totally obvious that she had neglected to take care of her car. All extended warranties and factory warranties spell it out: Maintenance neglect is not covered. So not only did she almost kill another car, but she was also stranded in a hotel room for several days, resulting in a huge repair bill plus a huge expense bill. Some people just never learn. You have to maintain your automobile or you risk invalidating your warranty.

Some of the lines you might hear from the finance manager when he is pitching extended warranty are what you have just read: "If you keep your cars for a long time . . . , if you drive high mileage . . . , if you travel . . . , and like having insurance, you'll have complete peace of mind in the event of a breakdown." Here's a really big one: "An extended warranty will increase the value of your automobile by at least five hundred when you are ready to trade again. The appraiser will know that your car has been taken really good care of and because it was covered under extended warranty, he will allow you more trade-in value thus recovering your cost of the extended warranty."

Some dealers use what's called a trade-in voucher to help boost the sale of extended warranties. When an extended warranty is purchased, the dealer will use trade-in vouchers to supposedly guarantee a specific dollar amount increase above the actual value of your trade-in. Both the dealer and the customer sign the vouchers at the time of sale. The idea behind these vouchers is that the next time you trade you show your sales representative the voucher and whatever amount it's filled out for is what you get extra for your trade-in. This would be a wonderful concept

> Quick, hand me my boots. It's gettin' deep!

if it were truly legitimate. Vouchers are just more fuel for their lines and another closing tool to get your cash. I used vouchers all the time and believe it or not, they worked on many. These vouchers are pulled out of the closet only as a last resort after several attempts have been made to sell an extended warranty and the customer repeatedly refuses. Two problems with vouchers are: 1. you must go back to the same dealer when you trade, and 2. when you do trade again, the dealer already knows up front that you have the voucher and how much it's made out for. (A copy of it is made and kept in your original purchase file.) When it's time to negotiate the price on your new purchase, the voucher amount is automatically figured into the deal and you've actually gained nothing—nada. It's basically a worthless piece of hype. Extended warranties/service contracts are marked up just like credit insurance except that the price can be negotiated down.

They are marked up as much as the finance manager can get away with. Here's how dealers make their profit on them. Dealers agree to sell extended warranties/service contracts through the company of their choosing. They will have a set cost to them on each plan based on what the category or class of the vehicle. Whatever price a dealer decides to sell the warranty over and above that cost is pure profit. Some of the manufacturers set and regulate the price of the extended warranty for dealers and they are supposed to abide.

However, dealers don't always follow directions. One customer where the sale made a good profit on the front end might buy a five-year/60,000 mile extended warranty for $700 with a cost to the dealer of $200 (a profit of $500). The very next customer, who happened to negotiate a great deal on the front end and whose

Warranties are marked up as much as the finance manager can get away with.

vehicle falls into the same category or class, might be charged $1,200 (a profit of $1,000) for the exact same plan. The sales manager will be frustrated with this customer because there was very little profit made on the front end. Therefore, the finance manager is instructed to draw blood. Actually, the finance manager will always try to draw blood, but even more so if there wasn't much profit made on the actual sale of the vehicle. The main things to remember are to identify those lines when they are being pitched, determine if you really are a candidate for extended warranty, and, finally, know that the price is without question negotiable. Dealers will argue with you until they're blue in the face on that one. They will swear up and down that they can't negotiate the price, but they can!

> If you're purchasing a used unit, it's a gamble.

Understand Your Factory Warranty

Understanding your factory warranty completely will certainly help in deciding what type of (if any) extended warranty plan to get should you give in and buy one. Always take into consideration how much factory warranty comes with your automobile. Once again, if you are leasing or only going to keep your vehicle for a short term, then honestly, I wouldn't worry about it unless you're a high mileage driver. And even then, what are the chances of a major mechanical breakdown? Slim to none! Plus, on a new automobile, customers have the first twelve months or 12,000 miles to decide if they really want to buy an extended warranty, so don't get caught up in their power of persuasion game. There's no rush! You do not have to buy right away. By the end of the first year or 12,000 miles you'll know if you're going to need it. Your car's performance will tell all!

History will usually repeat itself when it comes to automobiles.

Check with the Service Department

With the increased competition among manufacturers, the overall quality of all new automobiles has vastly improved in the last ten years. Check with the dealership service department prior to purchasing your automobile and ask questions about the reliability of the make you are considering. That could be a big determining factor in choosing to buy an extended warranty. If you are buying a used automobile, whether it be a certified unit, program unit, or previously owned unit by an individual, get the VIN number before making a purchase and have a service department that handles that particular line run a complete service check on it.

Go with Reputable Companies Only

For both new and used automobiles, if the extended warranty plan you're being offered is not one of the automotive manufacturer programs such as GMPP (General Motors Protection Plan), Acura Care, Chrysler Service Contract, Ford ESP (Extended Service Plan), or Honda/Easy Care, then whatever you do, don't buy it, period! Too many times customers will buy a warranty plan that is backed by an independent company or the dealer and, before they know it, that company/dealer has either been bought out or has gone bankrupt. This means months and months of legal litigation and reorganization. If you're one of those customers and you happen to have a mechanical problem, you've wasted your money! You have a worthless contract and have lost every single penny you invested in the warranty plan. Another scenario would be if you were traveling out of state somewhere and broke down. I feel sorry for you. If you're lucky, just *maybe* the warranty company will approve your repairs (one week after you've racked up a huge hotel and expense bill), but most likely not. Take my word for it, please.

Comprehensive Coverage

Automobiles no longer consist of your basic engine, transmission, and drive axle. They are much more complicated and technical than ever before. In fact, it would be safe to say that they largely operate on computer components. That's why automobiles are so expensive and costly to repair. For this reason, if you do choose to buy an extended warranty, get the most comprehensive coverage that you need for your vehicle.

If your car has it, cover it. If it doesn't have it, don't cover it. Don't let the dealer undersell you or oversell you. It's that simple—get what you need and if it's not included but offered, add travel expense (hotel and meals), roadside service, and towing. You want the most benefit for your money and if you have to spend a little extra, it's worth it. If you are gonna do something, do it right.

I recently had to deal with a problem that involved an extended warranty. On the last automobile I purchased, I was offered it four times and four times I declined. I knew that I had time to make my decision. I also knew that the manufacturer would be soliciting me through the mail and also over the phone. Shortly after purchasing my car, I received a bill in the mail for $1,300 for an extended warranty that I supposedly bought. You talk about going through the roof, I was furious!

The next day I called the warranty company and informed them that I had not purchased any such plan and I wanted to know why I was billed for it. The lady I spoke with told me that the dealer had turned my name in as buying it and that I would have to call the dealer. I

If the warranty isn't backed by a reputable company, don't buy it!

> Cover every
> component
> that your
> vehicle
> has—no
> more and
> no less.

told her to cancel the warranty immediately because I was not going to pay for it. After hanging up the phone with her, I called the dealer and asked to speak with the finance manager. Of course he wasn't there (yeah, right) so I spoke with his assistant. When I told him what the problem was, he claimed that it was a computer error and not to worry about it. He said that it would cancel itself out if I did not pay for it.

Well, I took them (the dealer and the warranty company) at their word and trusted that the situation would soon be resolved. Not so! Thirty days after receiving the first bill, I received yet another one along with a late notice. This bill was for $1,300 plus late charges. I think every hair on my body stood straight up I was so angry. Again, I called the warranty company and the dealer, and they gave me the same runaround for the second time. I demanded to both parties that the warranty be cancelled immediately. I never purchased it and I was not about to pay for it!

Several months passed and still the situation had not been resolved. Each month I received a notice from the warranty company. They would demand payment, and every month I had to call them and go through the same ridiculous routine. (This is yet another one of those obscure and harassing games that dealers play on unsuspecting customers—all in the name of greed.) I tried to be very patient but when I started getting collection letters, that did it! I finally had to threaten all parties with legal action before getting any satisfaction. Then and only then was the service contract cancelled and the bill deleted.

This happens to so many customers every year. They buy an automobile that is eligible for extended warranty and then the dealer tries to sell them on some sort of plan. No matter how many times a customer declines and regardless of whether they bought a plan or not, the dealer assumes that they will eventually buy and the customer's name is reported to the warranty company as having bought something. This is called assumptive selling. Within a few months, the customer is billed for a grossly overpriced extended warranty plan and is given the opportunity to make payments rather than pay for it in one lump sum. If the customer doesn't buy on the first go around, the monthly billing will continue until they either give in or threaten legal action like I had to do. This approach is used in hopes that customers will change their mind and eventually go ahead with a purchase. When they do, the dealer scores once again.

As you can see, dealers can really slam-dunk unsuspecting customers, not only on the front end of a sale but on the back end as well, months down the road. It doesn't matter how demeaning, deceptive, or harassing they are to their customers. They just want their money any way they can get it. Add up all of the profit made from interest rate, credit life, accidental health insurance, and extended warranty and the total can run into the thousands. Now add that total to the profit made on the actual sale. Breathtaking isn't it? It doesn't have to be that way.

Take control. Negotiate the best purchase price, negotiate the trade-in value, negotiate the best lease, negotiate the interest rate, and negotiate the extended warranty. Negotiate everything! That's the only way to buy!

Legal Requirements on Automotive Insurance

Automotive insurance is not something of a choice. It's the law! Anyone driving at all is required to have automotive insurance, and if you don't abide and get caught driving without it, you could get into a lot of trouble. That's a major no-no! You could be ticketed and fined, have your license revoked, or, if you're involved in any kind of accident, you could be taken directly to jail.

There are many factors that determine what an individual's insurance rate (cost) will be: sex (male or female), marital status, age, the number of drivers that will be covered under your policy and their ages, where you work and how many miles you drive to and from work daily, what state and area in that state you live in, whether you had insurance cancelled before for non-payment or any other reason, the type of automobile (sedan, coupe, sports, luxury, truck, van, SUV, etc.), the age, make, and model of your automobile, the color of your automobile, safety features, whether your car will be garaged, whether it is financed or leased, your driving record, and any driver's education defensive driving courses taken.

The actual amount of automotive insurance required depends on the state you live in and whether or not your automobile is paid for or financed/leased. If you owe a balance, the creditor (lender) would require you to obtain full coverage maintaining in effect at least the minimum insurance coverage on public liability, physical damage, collision, and comprehensive with fire and theft prior to delivery. You would also be required to provide the creditor a copy of your insurance policy listing them as the loss payee. In the event of a loss (a wreck, fire, flood, etc.), the creditor would collect the proceeds from the insurance company and apply the settlement towards either the replacement of the vehicle or payment of the obligation.

To give you a better understanding of what each insurance covers, here is a list:

1. **Collision** Covers damages to your own car if it is involved in a collision regardless of whose fault it is. There may be a deductible.

2. **Comprehensive** For the noncollision losses to your automobile such as fire, theft, flood, hail, vandalism, glass breakage, etc. There may also be a deductible.

3. **Liability** Covers bodily injuries, death, or property damages caused by your automobile.

4. **Medical Payment** Pays medical expenses no matter whose fault it is (you or occupants in your automobile).

Note: One additional type of coverage that I would recommend to everyone who has an automobile financed is the gap insurance I spoke of earlier. If an automobile were totaled, the gap protection would cover any remaining balance left on a loan after an insurance settlement.

Even though liability insurance (bodily injury, property damage, and medical payment) is the only requirement if your automobile is paid for, it is far better to have that safety net with full coverage and protect everyone and everything around you, including yourself. You may be the best driver in the whole entire world, but all it takes is one second and one reckless, drunk, high, or aggressive driver to wipe out and kill. The cost of full coverage insurance is extremely cheap when compared to life. Don't risk lives by being a miser.

When you get behind that wheel, drive to live, not die.

If you're involved in an automobile accident, it's always best to contact the police immediately, no matter how minimal the damages are. You never know the full extent until after the dust has settled. You might have sustained injuries that won't show up until later, or the damages to your automobile may be more severe than it appears. Once the police officer gives you a temporary copy of the accident report, contact your insurance company as soon as possible. After you report the accident to your insurance company, they will file the insurance claim for you. You will need to provide them with an official accident report, which is usually available within a few days after the incident.

The thing we all want to remember is to drive as safely as possible. The safer we drive, the less automobile accidents, deaths, and injuries there will be.

We hear the following everyday but take it for granted and pay no attention. We say, "Oh, it will never happen to me." It only takes a split second before you or your loved ones are on the way to the hospital in an ambulance, seriously injured or dead. You have to realize that you're not only driving for yourself but for everyone else that's behind the wheel. You're driving for your safety and their

Please do your part in protecting your loved ones, yourself, and those around you, including other drivers. The responsibility belongs to all of us . . .

safety. You can't control other drivers but you can control what you do and how you respond to them, whether they are in front of you, next to you, or behind you. If you would, make a copy of the following, "Driving For Life." Keep it on your refrigerator and occasionally read it as a reminder. These simple little suggestions will help you become more aware of what's going on around you, thus making you a safer driver.

Driving for Life

Before you even get in your vehicle, leave your troubles and worries outside! Do not bring them to the wheel. They cause distractions, poor judgment, and aggressiveness. Next, put that seatbelt on and lock those doors! Never go anywhere without fastened seatbelts and locked doors. So many people have been killed because they didn't wear their seatbelt or their doors were unlocked and they got attacked or car-jacked. By having the doors locked, that will allow you more time to escape.

Don't rush. Five minutes isn't going to make a bit of difference no matter where you are going. If other drivers are crowding you on the road or rushing you, then slow down and let them pass. Keep your distance until they are gone.

When it first begins to rain, be cautious of the road conditions. There's oil build-up on the roads and they are extremely slippery at first until the rain has had a chance to wash the oil away. If you see water puddles in the road, slow down. They may be deeper than you think and can cause you to hydroplane. If there is any kind of moisture whatsoever (rain, sleet, snow, or ice) on the roads, take your time and be extremely careful. Wear sunglasses to guard against sun glare.

Watch out for all of God's creatures, big and small. They deserve to live too! Slow down if you see anything that looks unusual ahead of you. If drivers in front of you are hitting their brakes repeatedly, you do the same. There's probably a reason for it. Do not get so close to the drivers in front of you that you're riding their bumper. They might stop suddenly. If there are pedestrians near the street, please slow down. You don't want to accidentally hit one of them.

Even if you're approaching a green light, slow down at intersections. You never know when someone is going to run a red light. If you see someone on a side street waiting to pull onto the main road that you're traveling on, slow down. They might not see you and pull out in front of you.

If you become sleepy or tired at all, roll the windows down and get some fresh air until you can pull over and stop. Splash cold water on your face and get some caffeine into your system. If you can't have caffeine, run around your car about ten times.

Abide by all of the driving laws! They are implemented to protect you, not hurt you. And finally, please, please, please don't drink and drive.

DRIVE FOR LIFE, YOU'RE WORTH IT

I mentioned that my father had been a published author. I have a folder of his work that I cherish dearly and I would like to share some of it with you that was published in the *Strategian*, a military publication. (He was in the Air Force). At the time I was writing this particular chapter, I had no idea that my dad had written the piece that follows. As I got the idea of incorporating some of his work into my book as a memoriam gesture, I began thumbing through the folder and found "Slow Down, Live."

I thought it was strangely coincidental and interesting that he wrote, "Slow Down, Live" and I wrote "Driving For Life," especially since I had never read it. He was always emphasizing the importance of safety no matter what you were doing. This is for you, Daddy.

Slow Down, Live
By S.Sgt. Keith E. Lyle
(Published August 1, 1963)

Come on now, set yourself down under the ole china-berry tree, stick that fishin' pole in the ground, take off your shoes and put your feet in that good ole muddy water. Now, light your pipe and we're ready.

I want to talk about safety. Huh, you say? We hear about safety at almost every Commander's Call and before almost every holiday we are forced to sit in the theater and look at a gory film.

Well, those little talks and films may have saved our lives without us even knowing it. We never really forget anything. It's just stored in the subconscious part of our minds until we need that particular bit of information and there it is ready to cause us to act, sometimes without even being conscious of its presence.

Personally, I am very grateful for these talks and films. But from the looks of Air Base Road and Sunset in the morning and afternoon, we sure need a lot more of them.

Some morning or afternoon drive Air Base Road at 50 miles per hour (the posted speed limit) and count the cars that pass you. I did, and in this small distance 22 cars passed at speeds in excess of 50 miles per hour.

Does this mean that 22 people have some kind of emergency that precludes them driving at a safe and prudent speed? I don't think so. I'm sure that the wife or NCOIC (whichever happens to be at the end of our journey) will understand if we are a few minutes late. But, I don't think our small children could understand and accept the fact that daddy can never come home again because someone likes to drive fast or was just plain careless.

God gave us all a sense of preservation, an ability to reason and understand danger. We learn from the time that we are little children that things can and will hurt us. But, sometimes we allow ourselves to fall into complacency and routine carelessness that can kill us and our loved ones. I would like to ask one question. Is it worth two minutes extra, twice a day—a total of four minutes a day—to increase your chances of being with your loved ones again? It's worth it to me.

Since we can't stay here at the ole fishin' hole indefinitely and the fish aren't biting anyway, I'll see you back at the base. But take it easy, huh? I'm not quite ready for any sad singin' and slow marchin'.

Don't drink and drive or take drugs and drive, and don't let any of your loved ones do it either, or you'll be knockin' at death's door.

I realize that the speed limit isn't 50 mph, but everything is relative. In the sixties when this was written, the speed limit was much slower than today. But the fact remains that we must continue to be safety conscious at all times, not only for ourselves, but for our loved ones and everyone else around us.

Here is a published poem he wrote that really hits hard. It's about drinking and driving . . .

The Devil Claims His Own
By S.Sgt. Keith E. Lyle

The big car rolled, with the greatest of ease,
Over hills and valleys, just like a breeze.
They all had a drink, before they left town,
Now they passed that bottle around.
The Devil said; Boys, you're having fun,
Enjoy those drinks, each and every one.
They drank that wildcat whiskey down,
Thinking their troubles, they would surely
    drown.
Over bridges and through canyons, and all
    the while,
Tires getting hotter, each and every mile.
Then on a curve there was a loud bang, a
    twist and a ravel,
And end over end that big car did travel.
Metal and glass, blood and guts,
Mixed with alcohol, there in the ruts.
Now these young hearts are stilled today,
There was no time to stop and pray.
'Cause when a man drinks the Devil's brew
    this way,
Sooner or later, he's got to pay.
DON'T DRINK AND DRIVE!

CHAPTER 11

Some Comments about Automobile Advertising

I t's 6:00 A.M. and all's quiet on the home front. You're just beginning to wake up as the bright new sunshiny day beams down upon your face through the window shades. You breathe in deeply and ahhh, the wonderful aroma of freshly brewed coffee filters through the air. You're feeling fantastic! Then suddenly, the radio alarm kicks in blaring the first voice you hear for the day. Annoying and obnoxiously loud, the announcer blurts out faster than a high-dubbed recording some commercial about some superduper automotive weekend sale at some dealership. What's worse is that when the commercial is over, you're not really sure what you heard.

You know something was said about great prices on selected models, low payments, low interest rates, and trade-in guarantees, but the actual particulars and requirements zoomed by even faster. You think you heard right, or did you? Maybe you heard wrong. Well, the advertisement did exactly what it was supposed to do. It attracted your attention and stirred up your curiosity enough that you jump in the car and go check it out. But what will the story be when you get there?

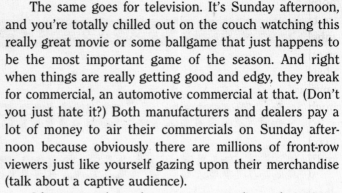

Is what you hear what you heard and is what you see what you get?

The same goes for television. It's Sunday afternoon, and you're totally chilled out on the couch watching this really great movie or some ballgame that just happens to be the most important game of the season. And right when things are really getting good and edgy, they break for commercial, an automotive commercial at that. (Don't you just hate it?) Both manufacturers and dealers pay a lot of money to air their commercials on Sunday afternoon because obviously there are millions of front-row viewers just like yourself gazing upon their merchandise (talk about a captive audience).

Of course, they always seem to show their most desirable and luxurious models in a most glamorous manner, all to entice you! Does it work? Yes, but in the last few seconds of the commercial as you're daydreaming about owning that automobile, television advertisements do the same thing radio ads do. You hear that all too familiar announcement at the end, but in a softer voice so as not to distract from the automobile's beauty. And on top of that, flashed up on the screen in tiny fine print are the particulars: down payment requirements, restrictions, and anything else you might need to know. The print is so small and goes by so quickly that it is impossible to read it. You think you know what you saw, and you kinda heard it, but if you go check it out, are you going to be disappointed?

While we're discussing advertising, we must include the newspapers, magazines, and sale flyers. Manufacturers and dealers use the same approach except it's all in assorted print. What they want you to notice is in giant bold print and what they don't want you to notice, you need a magnifying glass to see, let alone read.

Your curiosity got the best of you and now you're at the dealership. Are the superduper, specially priced automobiles the hot loaded up ones you thought they'd be or are they the plain-Jane versions with no options? Are the unbelievably low interest rates attainable for everybody or only for those with ten years of A-plus credit? Are the advertised monthly payments based on a minimum down payment or do you have to own a bank to make that much down payment? And about the advertised payment, is it a purchase payment or a lease payment? Are the guaranteed trade-in prices on new and used or just used? And? And?

Guaranteed trade-in allowance? No such thing!

Whether by radio, television, or print, there are disclosure and protection laws required when advertising. These laws protect against nonsubstantiation (not being able to back up what they claim), deception (false and misleading claims) and unfairness (being treated unfairly). If companies do not abide by these laws, they could end up with more legal problems than they bargained for. That's why automotive advertising is disclosed so quickly and in such fine, hard-to-read print. (They throw you just enough bait to catch your attention, then they reel you in. Dealers can't sell you anything if you're not caught in their net.)

If consumers could hear the whole truth, see the whole picture, and read the whole book, their desires and curiosity would go down, the success rates of these devious advertising tactics would drop, and sales would diminish. So wise up and don't believe everything you hear, see, or read. ADVERTISING CAN BE MISLEADING!!

Caveat Emptor: Let the Buyer Beware

Do your homework! Before you begin chasing some too good to be true ad you heard on the radio, saw on TV, or read in print, take the time to make some phone calls. It will only take a few minutes of your time. Find out the facts, the requirements, and the restrictions. Then if you're still enticed, go for it! But remember: You can't believe everything you hear, see, or read!

CHAPTER 12

You Are Ready to Hit the Lots

We're near the end so let's just quickly review a few things that I feel are very important to remember throughout the whole process of buying an automobile.

The Informed Buyer Attitude

Now you can truly say you're an informed buyer.

Oh, you're definitely informed all right. You have now been enlightened to things that management wouldn't dare teach the sales staff. It feels great doesn't it? Isn't it wonderful to know that for the rest of your car shopping days you'll have the upper hand and the power to prevent anyone from ever financially taking advantage of you? You have the knowledge and the know-how to prevent it from happening if you utilize what I've taught you in this book. I've given you everything I know, thirteen years of inside secrets, stories, and other extremely important information. I've exposed and confessed.

You know all the different options available in automobiles and the different classifications, new and used. You not only know all the different purchasing options available to you, but you understand the profit potential

Don't It
Make You
Wanna
Shout . . .

More sales
equals
higher per-
centage
equals mo'
money!

Negotiate
what?
EVERY-
THING!

behind each one. You know why a sales representative will continually call you to the point of harassment.

You know the relationship between manufacturers and dealerships and how important it is for dealers to keep their customers happy (Customer Service Index/CSI gets too low and they could lose their dealership). You know about the business and should have a complete understanding of sales, financing, leasing, trade-ins, credit insurance, and extended warranties.

You know all the little complexities that make up each and every phase of a sale, a finance deal, and a lease. You know the dealers' strategies and their many lines used to sell customers unnecessary snake oil and laha, croak, and choke. You understand about trade-ins, the best way to get their value, and how important it is to know their value before talking to any dealer. You know all about the different auctions and much more. But most importantly, you now know how to overcome dealers and win the absurd and unjust games they play. You definitely have a handle on *negotiating*!

It wouldn't hurt you one bit to read this book two or three times before venturing out. Then you can really strut your stuff, with a good attitude of course!

You must be careful about your attitude. Don't get too cocky and start acting like the know-it-all! Nobody likes a know-it-all. Utilize your newfound knowledge in a positive way. Be the informed buyer but listen to what the dealer has to offer and be open to suggestions. In the automotive world things change daily. If you go in with that know-it-all attitude, you're only going to cut your own throat. Be considerate, but be strong and confident. Keep the upper hand (control) and don't let your guard down. You can win this one!

Don't Be a Bully

No sales person wants to be intimidated by a bully. Leave the threatening and defensive attitudes at home. Do not agitate the dealer! That's not what this is all about. If you attack, you're asking for it. They will do their best to RIP YOUR HEAD OFF! So put your dukes down and leave the boxing to Don King and his pros. You can be strong and confident and stand your ground without any bullying around.

Good Golly Ms. Molly! Oh, excuse me, Mr. Molly. What are you doing?

Don't Be a Lay-Down

Grab the reins and lead the way! Don't say yes. Just say no until you get what you want or at least close to it. You and the dealer will eventually meet somewhere in the middle, maybe. I just hope it's closer to your middle than their middle. Remember that you don't have to finance or lease with them. You don't have to buy any snake oil (paint sealant, fabric protection, rustproofing, or undercoating). If the automobile is new, it was probably already applied at the factory. And credit insurance? Forget it, at least through the dealer or lender, and maybe even the credit union. It's good to have, but find yourself an insurance agent and save yourself some money. Do yourself a favor and don't buy any extended warranty unless you really need it. Before you buy it though, make sure you know exactly what kind of warranty you already have, if any.

JUST SAY NO!!

If you're "blinded by the light," you're gonna mess up big time!

Don't Fall in Love

Get over it! It's just a vehicle. There are too many fish in the sea to get lovesick. Take off your rose-colored glasses Miss Rosalie and see it for what it is. If you're blinded by the light, you're gonna mess up big time.

Not only that, it's going to hurt and you will feel the repercussions down the road! Don't rush into anything. Think about what you are doing, take your time, and don't be influenced by others. God gave you a brain—use it! Be selective; there are lots to choose from out there. Most importantly, don't settle for anything less than what is right for you. You deserve it!

You can't buy champagne on a beer budget!

Stick to Your Financial Limits

Did I say enough about financial limits? It is so very important to stay within your financial limits no matter what you are buying. You can't buy champagne on a beer budget.

It simply doesn't work! If you try it, you're not going to like it. You might enjoy it for a while, but eventually after the newness wears off, you'll realize how uncomfortable you are and see all of the other things you're missing out on. If you try to handle too much, ooh . . . what a hangover you're going to have. Do you want to drive through the valley of the shadow of financial despair?

Be Ready to Walk Away from a Bad Deal

If the dealer is playing cut-throat games with you and insists on his terms, then get up and walk out! You don't have to buy there. As in the frog and scorpion tale, there are too many scorpions out there waiting for their turn to ride across that pond. Both of you grab an oar and row, row, row—together. It's all up to you now.

No matter where you live or travel to, there's a scorpion waiting for you!

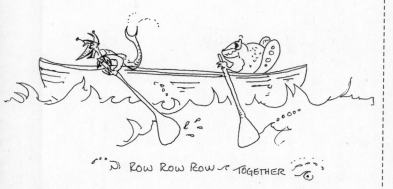

ROW ROW ROW TOGETHER

You're not the cowardly lion in *The Wizard of Oz*. You are strong so stand up and roar-r-r! You'll save thousands!

Final Thoughts and Words of Thanks

We finally made it to the end, and I hope you're still here with me! You truly are ready to hit the lots now and I'm so very proud of each of you for taking the time to read my book. I thank you with all of my heart! As I look back, after I quit the automotive business the thought of writing this book weighed heavily on my mind for a long time. It was like a thorn buried deep in my side and the pain just wouldn't go away. There were many sleepless nights that seemed to never end because I felt so bad about ripping people off. But it was expected of me; I was only doing my job.

I knew I couldn't go back in time and change the past, but maybe I could do something about the future. Then finally one day I did it. I sat down and began to write. I struggled and struggled with it for a long time because I knew this book had to be completely different from anything out there. I wanted it to be special, more than just another automotive book. I wanted to touch the hearts and souls of those who read it in such a way that it would truly make a difference. I wanted to give back what I took and share with others not only about the automotive business, but about the value of life and the importance of believing in oneself and never giving up.

A day without laughter is like a day without sunshine!

Again, the information contained in this book was drawn directly from my own experiences. I'm no big scholar with a bunch of plaques hanging on my walls, nor do I claim to be. I'm just a woman who gave thirteen long, hard years of her life to the auto industry. And what did I get in return? I gained self-respect and became self-sufficient. I learned to be strong and independent. And through perseverance, I conquered many trials and tribulations, including those I faced while working in the automobile business.

Above all, I learned to love myself, the greatest lesson of all! For you can't love others if you don't love yourself.

NO MATTER WHERE YOU LIVE, GO OR TRAVEL TO .... THERE'S A SCORPION ....
.... WAITING FOR YOU !!!!

Glossary of Terms

accidental health insurance Insurance that will pay in the event you get sick, hurt, or disabled for a period of time (there are many plans available). You must provide written proof from your physician.

acquisition fee Up-front dealer/lender charges for processing and handling a lease.

actual cash value The actual value of an automobile to a wholesaler or dealer.

addendum sticker The additional price sticker with added options and chemicals. It is usually placed next to the factory sticker. The dealer adds these items and sets the price of each.

add-ons The added options and chemicals listed on the addendum sticker. There are two types: hard add-ons are options, and soft add-ons are chemicals.

aftermarket products Options that can be added to a new or used automobile after it is purchased (pinstripes, tinted windows, sunroofs, stereos, etc.).

appraisal The evaluation of an automobile to find its true value.

arbitration The process wherein a settlement is made in arbitration court or by a licensed arbitrator between the dealer and the customer on a purchased vehicle that turned out to be a lemon.

auction An auction can be a private sale (for dealers only) or a public sale in which automobiles are sold to the highest bidder.

automotive pricing consulting services Businesses that offer assistance in finding the right vehicle at the right price for consumers. They will locate as well as negotiate. They also offer complete printouts listing the invoice (cost) and retail, all for a fee.

automotive club pricing services Any of the automotive clubs, such as AAA, that offers the same pricing services that the consulting services offer for an additional fee above the membership fee.

back end The financing or leasing part of a sale and the profit made on financing, leasing, credit insurance, extended warranty, and any other products sold in the finance office.

balloon note A contract in which smaller payments are made throughout the term of the loan with one final large payment, which makes up the deficit left from making the smaller payments.

base monthly payment The monthly lease payment including rate charge without usage (sales) tax.

black book One of the wholesale reference books the automotive industry uses to determine the value of an automobile.

bonus incentives The extra perks (money, trips, prizes, etc.) given to dealers and their sales force for accomplishing set goals and quotas.

budget The allotted amount of money you have or can afford for purchasing an automobile. This means not going over your limit.

buyer agents Agents that will actually do all of the negotiating for you from front to back, start to finish. All you have to do is pick out the vehicle you want and the buyer agent does the rest, for a fee.

buyer's remorse When you buy something and wake up the next morning wishing you hadn't bought it. Major regrets and anguish!

capitalized (cap) cost The best straight-out (no trade) purchase price on a lease.

capitalized cost reduction The down payment (cash, net trade-in—trade-in minus payoff, manufacturer rebates, and dealer incentives) that is deducted from the capitalized cost on a lease.

certificate of origin The original certificate that comes with each new automobile showing where it came from and what dealer bought it.

certified used cars These units have been through a 100-plus point inspection. They're reconditioned and put on the lot for sale. They are usually backed by some type of warranty.

charge back When a loan is paid off early, the profit that was made on interest rate and credit insurance is prorated and charged back to the dealer. This also applies to cancelled credit insurance and extended warranties.

closed-end lease This is a lease in which customers have two options:

1. At lease end, they can turn the leased vehicle back in and lease another one or walk away free and clear provided there are no penalty charges (excess mileage or excess wear and tear).
2. They can purchase the leased vehicle for the estimated residual value stated in their lease contract. A word of advice on purchasing your lease: Only purchase it if the value is the same as or less than the estimated residual value. You can sell it privately for a profit and then buy or lease a new one.

closer Someone whose primary job is to close a sale (convince a customer to buy before leaving the lot).

cobuyer Someone who enters into a joint purchase by financing. They are part owner and have the same responsibility of making payment in full as the principle buyer.

college graduate program A finance program available to students who have recently graduated from college or who will be graduating within the academic semester (they must have a diploma or some form of written verification).

commission A percentage of profit made on a sale that is paid to sales representatives for their services.

comparative shopping Negotiating the best purchase price on the same unit or units from different dealerships and comparing their prices.

conditioned approval When a customer is approved for a loan but there are conditions that must be met first, such as the down payment, restricted payment, etc.

conventional financing The general or ordinary finance contracts through banks, credit unions, and finance companies.

cosigner Someone who assists another person by lending their good credit and agreeing to sign on the finance contract. They are only looked to for payment if the principle buyer fails to make payments.

credit bureau A business that collects credit information on individuals and business from lenders on a regular basis. They will issue credit reports when requested, usually for a fee.

credit life insurance Life insurance that is sold and included in a finance contract that covers the debt in the event of a death.

credit report The reports that are retrieved from credit bureaus showing the payment history of an individual's or company's financial obligations.

customer satisfaction index (CSI) The rating on which quality of product and service to customers is based.

cyberworld The Internet.

dealer cost What the manufacturer charges the dealer for an automobile.

dealer reserve Profit a dealer makes off of interest charged.

dealer warranty Any warranty that is provided and backed by the dealer.

debt-to-income ratio The amount of debt one has versus the amount of income one makes.

demonstrator Any new or used automobile that is assigned to and driven by a dealer employer/employee as one of the job perks.

deposit Any money that is required to hold a particular unit so that no other customer can buy it.

depreciation The lost value of a unit during a given period of time.

destination charge The delivery charge on a delivered unit from the factory to the dealership.

discount To reduce the selling price.

disposition fee Lease-end dealer/lender charges for the disposal of a leased unit.

early termination Early payout on a contract.

equity The percentage of ownership that exceeds the liability (debt).

excess mileage charge A charge for any additional mileage driven in excess of the annual mileage allowance on a lease.

excess wear and tear Wear and tear on a leased unit beyond that which is acceptable by the lender/dealer.

executive unit Previously owned by the manufacturing companies and driven by their management executives.

extended warranty (service contract) Additional warranty that can be purchased.

fabric protection A protective coating applied to the fabric of an automobile.

factory warranty The warranty on a unit that is provided and backed by the manufacturer.

farm plan A financial plan that is available to farmers.

federal buyer's guide A form that is placed on the window of any used automobile stating the condition of warranty at sale. Example: As-Is No Warranty, or 3 MO/3,000-mile warranty.

finance To purchase by making payments over a period of time.

finance term The number of months for which one finances.

first-time buyer program A finance program for anyone who has never financed an automobile before.

floorplanning Factory finance companies and other lending institutions supply funds to dealers for their inventory.

front end The actual sale and the profit made on the sale.

gap protection Insurance on a lease to cover the gap between what an individual's auto insurance would pay and what the lease buyout would be (including early termination penalties) if a leased unit is totaled, stolen, or has physical damage prior to lease end. Also applies to a conventional loan and the payoff.

general maintenance The required care of an automobile, such as changing of fluids and filters. Refer to the owner's manual for your particular automobile.

grace period The number of days after the due date you have to make a payment until it is considered past due.

gross capitalized cost The best straight-out (no trade) purchase price plus any additional items you pay for over the lease term (such as extended warranties, insurance, and any outstanding prior credit or lease balance).

holdback Bonus or kickback money that automotive manufacturers award dealers on each new unit they sell, primarily to help pay for overhead and advertising.

incentives Bonuses, rebates, trips, prizes, etc. offered to increase sales.

in-house programs Finance or lease programs that a dealer handles internally.

in-service date The actual day a new unit is placed into demo service. The factory warranty goes into effect this date.

interest The charge for borrowed money.

interest rate The percent charged on borrowed money.

inventory All of the units (new and used) a dealer will have in stock.

invoice Dealer cost.

Kelley Blue Book An automotive price guide that lists wholesale, retail, and loan values.

lease A contracted agreement between a lender (lessor) and a customer (lessee) in which the lessee pays for usage of a vehicle owned by the lessor over a period of time.

lease term The number of months for which one leases.

lemon law The law that protects consumers in which they may take legal steps towards arbitration if they have purchased a car that is a "lemon." This law may vary from state to state.

lenders Those that loan money for a profit in return: banks, finance companies, credit unions, lease companies, etc.

lessee The customer.

lessor The lender or dealer.

liability insurance Bodily injury, property damage, and medical payment.

line 5'd A contract in which the customer is restricted in the amount of money that can be borrowed.

loan value The value of an automobile on which a loan is based. The amount that a lender will go over loan value is based on a customer's credit.

locator A computer service utilized by dealers to locate a particular vehicle that a customer wants to buy.

manufacturers The companies that build our automobiles.

market value Actual cash value; wholesale value.

meet and greet The beginning stages of a sale in which the sales representative gets to know the customer. Part of the pre-qualifying stage.

mini-deal A sale where there is very little profit made; therefore, the sales person is paid a minimum guaranteed commission.

money factor The lease rate (comparable to the finance rate) determined by the lender.

Monroney sticker The manufacturer's sticker that lists the equipment, MSRP, and other pertinent information.

monthly usage tax Sales tax paid on each base monthly payment of a lease.

MSRP Manufacturer's suggested retail price.

Official N.A.D.A. Used Car Guide An automotive price guide that lists retail and loan value.

negotiate Come to terms or come to an agreement on price.

net capitalized cost Gross capitalized cost minus capitalized cost reduction.

open-end lease This is a lease in which customers have two options:

1. At lease end, they can turn the leased vehicle back in but must pay any difference in the actual current residual value and the estimated residual value stated in their lease contract plus any and all penalties for excess wear and tear and excess mileage.
2. They can purchase the leased vehicle for the actual current residual value.

These are bad news! Don't even consider an open-end lease! It could cost you several thousands.

options The standard or optional equipment on a vehicle.

paint sealant A protective coating applied to the paint of an automobile.

payoff The balance on a loan minus prorated interest.

principle buyer The main buyer.

prequalify When a sales representative attempts to find out as much information as possible about a customer and their needs, desires, and financial capabilities.

product brochures The pamphlets or booklets containing pictures, charts, graphs, and other information on the different models of each automobile. Available at dealerships.

program unit Units sold through auctions that were pre-owned by rental companies, fleet companies, or lease companies.

purchase option fee A fee paid along with the residual value in the event a customer decides to purchase their lease. This fee is set by the individual lender.

qualified buyer A customer that meets certain conditions and requirements.

qualifications The conditions and requirements a customer must meet for approval.

rebates Cash back or refunds that are deducted from an amount to be paid or a return of part of an amount already paid.

Regulation M Effective January 1, 1998, Regulation M (*Federal Consumer Leasing Act Disclosures*) is the federal law requiring dealers and lenders to fully disclose all costs of a lease.

In the past, dealers and lenders were not required to disclose costs.

residual Estimated or projected value of a vehicle at the end of a lease determined by the individual lender.

retail value Street value, any amount over wholesale is actually retail. There is no set price, only a suggested value (manufacturer's suggested retail price).

roadside assistance A roadside service provided in the event of an automotive breakdown due to mechanical failure, flat tire, etc. Coverage depends on the company, but usually pays for towing and includes a twenty-four-hour helpline. Lodging and food expense is sometimes covered as well.

rustproofing A protective coating that is applied to the underside of an automobile.

security deposit Up-front deposit required, usually equal to the monthly lease payment rounded to the next twenty-five-dollar increment.

service contract (extended warranty) Additional warranty that can be purchased.

spot delivery Delivery of an automobile prior to customer financial approval.

stock Inventory.

street value Retail value.

superstore Dealer lots with huge, high-quality inventories such as AutoNation USA, CarMax, Car America, and SmartCars.

test-driving Driving an automobile to see how it rides, runs, and handles.

total of base monthly payments The depreciation of a leased unit plus rate charge.

total monthly payment The monthly lease payment including rate charge with usage (sales) tax.

trade-in allowance The amount allowed or given on a trade.

T.O. When a customer is turned over to another sales representative or a closer in an attempt to close a sale.

undercoating A protective coating that is applied to the underside of an automobile.

units Automobiles.

up-front deposit A requested deposit before any negotiations take place (cash, checks, credit cards, driver's license, etc.)

VIN Vehicle identification number.

walkaround Walking a customer completely around an automobile pointing out all of its features and benefits, inside and out.

wholesale value Actual cash value.

A Special Invitation

I am delighted to have had the opportunity to share this information with you. I welcome all of your letters and comments, good or bad. I'd love to hear from you. Tell me how and what part or parts of my book were most helpful with your next automotive purchase. How much money were you able to save and did you finance, lease, or perhaps pay cash? Maybe something in my book touched more than your pocket. Did it have a positive impact on your personal life? I would hope so, and I would hope that you'd share it with me.

Give me the scoop on all of your stories and experiences and please, don't leave out a single detail. Tell me everything! I truly do care. Who knows, your response may lead to another book and possibly help someone else work through a hard situation. I thank you in advance with my deepest appreciation, and I wish you the very best in all that you do! Hugs and kisses to everyone, and don't forget to laugh!

Love yourself—if you don't, no one else can!

PK Lyle
PO Box 460
Royersford, PA 19468
e-mail: PKLyle@netscape.net

Index

U

Universal joints in used car, 64
Up-front deposits, negotiating, 74–76
USA, 47
Used car lots. *See* Used cars
Used cars, 22–23, 41–43
   advantages of, 42
   at auctions, 45–47
   buying at buy-here pay-here lots, 49–50
   buying at independent lots, 48–49
   buying at superstores, 47
   certified, 42–43
   at dealerships, 45–47
   disadvantages of, 42–43
   extended warranties on, 42
   extended warranty on, 140
   getting true value of, 25
   retail value of, 84–86
   wholesale value of, 83–84
Used cars checklist
   air conditioners, 51
   battery, 51
   belts, 52
   brake fluid leakage, 52
   brakes, 52
   carburetor, 52
   catalytic converter, 52
   clipping, 53
   clutch, 53
   components, 53
   constant velocity joints, 54
   cooling system, 53–54
   crank shaft, 54
   doors, 54–55
   electrical system, 55
   emergency brake, 55
   empty containers, 55
   engine problems, 56
   exhaust, 56
   flood car, 56
   floor mats, 56
   fluids, 56–57
   front-wheel drive, 57
   gaskets, 57
   hood shocks, 57
   hoses, 57
   liftgate and trunk shocks, 57
   lighter, 57
   mileage rollback, 58–60

   motor mount, 60–61
   muffler, 61
   paint, 61
   previous driver, 61
   radiator, 61–62
   real-wheel drive, 62
   shocks and struts, 62
   stars in the windshield, 62–63
   steering, 63
   stereo system, 63
   tires, 63
   title brand, 63–64
   transmission, 64
   universal joints, 64
   vacuum lines, 65
   valve seals, 64
   water leaks, 65
   wrecked unit, 65–66

V

Vacuum lines in used car, 65
Valve seals in used car, 64
Vehicles. *See* Cars
VIN number (vehicle identification number), 4, 59, xxiv
Volkswagen, supply and demand for new, 1–2
Voucher, trade-in, 143–44

W

Walkaround, 28
Warranties
   coverage of, 42–43
   extended, 139–49
   factory, 37–38, 39, 140, 145
Water leaks in used car, 65
Wholesale value, 83–84
Windshield, stars in the, 62–63
Women as car salespeople, 9–10
Wrecked unit, 65–66

About the Author

PK Lyle was born in Shreveport, L.A. She joined the retail automotive world to finance her college education and ended up spending thirteen years in the industry. She has worked in virtually every aspect of the car sales business, as sales representative, finance manager, title clearance processing manager. Her daily routine included negotiating car deals, closing sales, training and managing sales teams, conducting daily and weekly sales meetings, appraising automobiles and purchasing new and used inventory.

PK Lyle built Finance and Insurance Department programs for car dealers and was effective in convincing customers to finance with the dealer instead of their own bank or credit union. She knew how to increase customer payments from $200 a month to $400 a month by selling life and accidental, health insurance, extended warranties, and after market products such as undercoating, rust-proofing, paint sealant. Eventually she could no longer be part of the car dealership world and ripping off people buying cars. She now works in the entertainment industry. She is married and the mother of four children.